WILD TURKEY MUSINGS

To those who share
their whiskey.

RARE BIRD 101

5TH ANNIVERSARY

WILD TURKEY MUSINGS

A WHISKEY WRITER'S RETROSPECTIVE

DAVID JENNINGS

CONTENTS

Contents

FOREWORD
BY FRED MINNICK

With the growth of bourbon, a new type of writer was born—the American whiskey writer. Our godfather is the great Chuck Cowdery, a Kentucky Bourbon Hall of Famer, who's been covering the whiskey industry since the 1990s. If not for Chuck breaking ground, the American whiskey writer specialist wouldn't exist. Before Chuck, nobody focused solely on bourbon. And since his blog grabbed the industry by the neck, we've seen writers, bloggers, vloggers, and now influencers come and go.

Yeah, everybody thinks they want to cover bourbon, feeding into this thought that it's a dream job—which it is—that's littered with rare bourbon samples—which it's not. To be in these ranks requires rolling up your sleeves, digging into archives, and interviewing *real* people who work at distilleries, not just the marketers or brand ambassadors. It requires separation from the joy and hobby of bourbon, and a laser focus into the business. And above all, you need passion to tell a story that nobody else can tell.

That's what David Jennings, a.k.a. Rare Bird, has done in his bourbon-loving journey.

When David's blog was introduced to me, I noticed he only covered Wild Turkey, and I immediately thought the concept was different and could be a great success. But blogging means showing up every day and creating content. How could he manage to do that covering only one brand?

Fortunately, Wild Turkey offers much opportunity for prose. But it wasn't Jimmy or Eddie Russell that made David's work special. Rare Bird's attention to detail and ability to write about what people, like me, want to read is what separates David from the rest of the pack. And there's one blog post he wrote in 2017 that, in my opinion, lifted Rare Bird into another flock of writers.

The post was titled "Wild Turkey Kentucky Spirit (1994 'Pewter-Top')," and the first paragraph illustrated a new talent in American whiskey writing:

> *Two years after the eight-year age statement was dropped from domestic Wild Turkey 101 in 1992, a promising new expression started hitting the shelves— Wild Turkey Kentucky Spirit. Unlike the retired American stalwart, Wild Turkey 101 eight-year, and its sly replacement, Old No. 8 Brand, Kentucky Spirit was released as a super-premium, single-barrel bourbon whiskey (at the familiar 101 proof, of course). While still lacking an age statement, Kentucky Spirit had just about everything else: a fancy bottle with a fancy pewter top, fancy packaging, and for the first time to my knowledge, fancy handwritten barrel and warehouse identifiers. It's quite obvious (at least in my opinion) that Kentucky Spirit was created to compete specifically with another well-known super-premium bourbon—Blanton's.*

What David accomplished in this opening paragraph is not taught in journalism school, and is what separates the good from the great in the modern era. He brought forth a high level of geekdom, while injecting his own theory and relating it to the individual fan. This is American whiskey writing at its finest, and *Wild Turkey Musings* is littered with this brilliant style. But it's David's journey to this book I want to discuss.

David Jennings began as a Wild Turkey "Super Fan," became a part-time blogger, left his banking job after writing his first book, *American Spirit*, and transitioned into a full-time whiskey author. David has become one of our most powerful whiskey voices and would pour anything out of his bar for a thirsty Wild Turkey fan.

But most importantly, his voice is echoed throughout the world and inside the warehouses of Lawrenceburg, Kentucky. You'll hear people quoting warehouse locations and details on particular Turkey releases. Most of the time, these facts originated on Rare Bird's blog.

Today, you'll get a deeper dive into that blog and more insight from the man who put Wild Turkey on his shoulders and told their story. I recommend pouring a little Turkey to sip alongside reading these pages. And be fully warned: this book may lead to more Wild Turkey purchases and a deeper enthusiasm for a hobby you already love.

Who knows, you may be inspired to start your own blog, launch a YouTube channel, or write a book. By the time you do, though, Rare Bird will probably have a Wild Turkey warehouse named after him.

The great ones always have something in bourbon named after them.

FRED MINNICK

PROLOGUE

B logs die; it's inevitable. At some point in time, be it the result of new-fangled technology, personal calamity, old age, or straight up disinterest, I must face the reality that my blog, *Rare Bird 101*, will one day end. It's not something I desire or look forward to, but I accept its finite existence. All the same, I don't have to accept that my passion for Wild Turkey bourbon and rye whiskey might be lost forever. Blogs die, books slumber.

In the mid-2010s, thanks to the generosity of a kind internet stranger, my whiskey journey veered in a direction I never expected or prepared for. I was introduced to vintage Wild Turkey bourbon, or "dusties," as we enthusiasts like to call the older, rarer bottles. The flavor profile was mesmerizing, and from the very first nose and sip, I was determined to learn everything I could about this wonderful spirit. And so, it began.

In the Fall of 2016, I posted my first whiskey review to RareBird101. com. It was short and to the point, but it was a start. Seemingly overnight, I was hooked on writing about whiskey.

It's hard to believe I've been blogging about Wild Turkey for over five years (squeezing out my first book, *American Spirit: Wild Turkey Bourbon from Ripy to Russell*, in the interim). All the while, the encouragement I've

1

received from the whiskey community has been overwhelming. From email subscribers and social media followers, to Kickstarter backers and Patreon supporters, I've been welcomed in the warmest of ways.

November 30, 2021, marked the fifth anniversary of *Rare Bird 101*. In celebration of that milestone, as well as ensuring some of my favorite Wild Turkey musings survive the collapse of the internet, I decided a paper-bound retrospective was in order. Consider it a mixtape of booze-focused composition.

Within these pages, you'll find my thoughts and opinions on select whiskey expressions, facts and fables of Wild Turkey history, pseudo-scientific comparisons, adventurous blends, countdowns, cocktails, and bits of ranting and raving scattered throughout. However, this isn't a simple compilation of published blog posts. Like it or not, you'll also be getting my commentary, including information, insight, and oddities about each entry. Some posts have anecdotes, others carry personal meaning, but if there's something to be said, I've endeavored to say it. I should also note that I've removed numerical ratings from the whiskey reviews in this collection. With only a handful of reviews represented, numerical ratings would lack relativity and perspective.

Thank you for opening this book. Whether you purchased it new in 2022, or found it tattered and covered in dust in 2042, your eyes not only keep my words alive but also the legacy of Wild Turkey and the Russell family. There are few bourbon brands with stories worthy of print, and even fewer as deserving as Wild Turkey. It's my hope that you find my ramblings entertaining, educational, and—with a little luck (or nip of whiskey)—inspiring. So, pour a glass and settle in as I guide you through five exciting years of *Wild Turkey Musings*.

10 Reasons To Sip Russell's Reserve Single Barrel Bourbon

I wrote much of this piece sitting in the lobby of an auto repair shop in Aiken, South Carolina. It was an extended lunch break from work, and with two small kids at home, free time to write was a luxury. Several months later, I recorded an episode of the Bourbon Pursuit podcast with Kenny Coleman, and this post came up as a talking point. Reading back over it, my writing style seems alien, yet the ten points hold true. Even in 2022, it's hard to beat Russell's Reserve Single Barrel Bourbon. dj

JUNE 22, 2017

Frustrated with coming home empty handed from dusty hunting? Feeling regret for trading away Grandpa's old Wild Turkey bottle? Or maybe you arrived late to the scene to find there's no dusty Turkey to be found anywhere? Well, you're not alone.

But there is hope. While dusty Wild Turkey 101 is truly special and deserving of praise, Russell's Reserve Single Barrel Bourbon is, in many ways, the equivalent of 101's classic past. As far as I'm concerned, it virtually "checks all boxes." Please allow me to elaborate as I count down *Ten Reasons You Should Be Sipping Russell's Reserve Single Barrel Bourbon.*

10. VERSATILITY. Anything a straight whiskey can do, Russell's Reserve Single Barrel can do well. Cocktails? For sure. It has the richness and spice to outperform most bourbons in the super-premium tier. On the rocks? Absolutely. While not my preferred way to sip, Russell's Reserve Single Barrel is full bodied and strong enough to maintain enjoyable flavor as the ice melts. Neat? *Are you kidding me?* Russell's Reserve Single Barrel shines best when sipped neat! A single straight pour is a journey down classic Wild Turkey Lane and always a memorable experience.

9. A TRUE SINGLE BARREL. There's something to be said about a quality single-barrel Kentucky straight bourbon. You can't batch its imperfections away. Russell's Reserve Single Barrel Bourbon is what it is; what comes from the barrel is what you sip, save for a touch of water to maintain the brand's 110 proof. For the consumer, that means each bottle (so long as they're from different barrels) has the potential to provide its own unique and rewarding experience.

8. PROOF. With a barrel-entry proof of 115, bottling a perfectly aged straight bourbon at 110 proof means you'll likely get a minimally diluted whiskey (maturation location depending). This is one of the factors that made vintage Wild Turkey 101 so flavorful—a bottling proof (101) close to barrel entry-proof (107, prior to 2004). A higher proof also makes Russell's Reserve Single Barrel more versatile (see reason 10).

7. AVAILABILITY. Most local retailers stocking super-premium whiskeys carry Russell's Reserve Single Barrel Bourbon (that goes for states with controlled alcohol retailing too). But if your local bottle shop isn't stocking Russell's Reserve, the store should be able to get the whiskey easily through their distributor. It can also be found online at nearly every major spirits vendor with a half-decent selection. The point being, it's available practically everywhere.

6. AFFORDABILITY. With a suggested retail price of $50, Russell's Reserve Single Barrel is one hell of a deal. I've seen it on sale as low as $35 and as high as $60 (store and state depending). If you see it for less than $40 in today's crazy bourbon marketplace, it's a no-brainer buy. And even at $60 a bottle, I'd still argue it's a solid bargain. There are very few (and I mean *very few*) single-barrel, higher proof bourbons that can compete at the same quality level for the same price.

5. CONSISTENCY. Each bottle of Russell's Reserve Single Barrel I've tasted to date has been of considerable quality with a similar core profile. Some are better than others, of course, but I've yet to have a sub-par experience. According to a March 29, 2017 Reddit AMA, Jimmy and Eddie Russell still taste every barrel that's bottled. That alone is likely the best reason to explain why Russell's Reserve Single Barrel is so consistent in quality.

4. NON-CHILL FILTERED. Chill filtering is a common process employed by distilleries as a method for removing residue. Its purpose is to make whiskey more visually appealing. Stated simply, it improves clarity by reducing cloudiness, thereby giving the spirit more of a clean metallic sheen. Russell's Reserve Single Barrel Bourbon bypasses this process.

There is great debate among whiskey enthusiasts as to the effects of chill filtration on flavor. While some believe it improves taste by removing fine particles (imperfections), most will argue that it's simply one more (unnecessary) step away from how the whiskey tasted straight from the barrel. I'm not sure about you, but I prefer my bourbon as unaltered as possible.

3. PRIVATE SELECTIONS. There's a lot of bourbon brands out there offering private barrel selections. The truth is, it's often hard to tell who selected what. Many of these selections come from NDPs (non-distiller producers) from which the whiskey is sourced from other (often undisclosed) distilleries. Russell's Reserve Single Barrel private selections come straight from Wild Turkey and are personally selected by distributors, retailers, or enthusiasts. Depending on the preferences and talents of the individuals sampling the barrels, profiles can vary from signature "on-profile" Wild Turkey to stunning "throwback" Wild Turkey (yes, even some coveted dusty notes are sometimes reported). And because these bottles typically carry a small retail premium (if any at all), there's very little investment risk over the standard non-select Russell's Reserve.

2. PROFILE. One of my favorite things about Russell's Reserve Single Barrel Bourbon is its unmistakably classic Wild Turkey profile. From rich core-bourbon notes, like vanilla, brown sugar, caramel, and oak, to a plethora of supportive notes, ranging anywhere from fruity to spicy, each bottle of Russell's Reserve Single Barrel offers its own tasting experience. And don't let the lack of an age statement deter you. It has complexity and balance that only comes from well-aged whiskey. According to interviews with the Russells, most barrels are typically pulled between eight to ten years of age (the proverbial "sweet spot" of bourbon maturity). Overall, the profile is somewhat of a paradox, as all Russell's Reserve tastes like Wild Turkey, yet each Russell's Reserve Single Barrel tastes distinctively unique.

1. IT'S WILD TURKEY. Clearly I'm biased on this one, but there's something to be said for an honest legacy. The once small-label Kentucky straight bourbon purchased by wholesaler Austin, Nichols & Co. in 1971 has turned into a worldwide mainstay thanks to the dedication and skill of Master Distiller Jimmy Russell. And with Eddie Russell formally named Master Distiller in 2015, there's been no true "changing of the guard." Jimmy's way is Eddie's way, and Eddie's got it down. Wild Turkey makes damn fine bourbon whiskey—has for decades now—and Russell's Reserve Single Barrel Bourbon is a modern-day testament to that legacy.

#1 IT'S WILD TURKEY

ILD TURKEY
ASTER'S
EEP 1894

Wild Turkey Master's Keep 1894

Some posts you never forget writing; this is one of them. I recall a mild feeling of dread after finishing my tasting notes for Master's Keep 1894. I was standing in my kitchen, staring in disbelief at an index card scribbled with sparse, uninspiring profile descriptors. *This was it? This was the best they could do?* Even worse, I had to write about it honestly and objectively.

As a diehard Wild Turkey fan, I found writing 1894's review no easy task. In fact, I stayed up until 1:00 AM to get it all down (on a work night, no less). Thankfully, I had just read an article about the making of the film *Tombstone* and how Kevin Costner walked away, leaving Kurt Russell to save it. With the success of *Dances with Wolves*, all eyes were on Costner's competing biopic, *Wyatt Earp*. As it turns out, the less historically accurate *Tombstone* stole the show. It was the angle I needed.

A few months later, I met Eddie Russell for the first time. I was nervous as hell. I wasn't just anxious about meeting someone I respected and admired in the industry; I was the smartass blogger that trashed Master's Keep 1894. As it turned out, he was cool as a cucumber. We sipped bourbon, talked single barrels, and never once did 1894 come up. It was an awesome thing. Too bad this whiskey ain't. dj

11

SEPTEMBER 6, 2017

B rew a pot of coffee or, better yet, pour yourself a generous dram of your favorite Wild Turkey because today I'm going to tell you a story. It's a story about bourbon, a story with all the typical trappings: nineteenth-century history, a beautiful rural Kentucky landscape, a coming of age, new discoveries, and a life-changing experience. And, unlike a lot of bourbon stories (far too many to name), I believe this one to be true. It's a story folks can relate to, especially those (like myself) who, in their youth, struggled to accept their future in the family business. Yet, as wonderful as the story may be, in the end it's about that very business. It's about selling bourbon.

This summer, Wild Turkey debuted the third release in the Master's Keep series—at least, the third release for Australians. That's right. Master's Keep 1894 is a limited-edition Kentucky straight bourbon whiskey exclusive to the Blokes and Sheilas in the Land Down Under. As *Saturday Night Live's* Kenan Thompson might ask, "What up with that?"

I'll get into the hows and whys later (or my best guess at them), but in the meantime let's focus on the backstory. I'll refrain from paraphrasing and let the liner notes from 1894's elegant box tell the tale (in Australian English):

Master's Keep 1894, the third expression in Master Distiller Eddie Russell's limited series of rare Kentucky Straight Bourbon Whiskies, honours the sacred place where he first fell in love with bourbon.

In 1894, Rickhouse A was the first structure built on top of Wild Turkey Hill, overlooking the mighty Kentucky River, and for over a century has reliably produced some of the world's finest whiskies. The strength of Rickhouse A lies in its elevation and exposure to the elements, which enable the bourbon to breathe and move freely through the barrel with the seasons.

In the summer of 1981, a distillery worker led a young Eddie Russell up the rickety stairs of Wild Turkey's oldest rickhouse to give him his first taste of whiskey straight from the barrel. It was then Eddie decided to dedicate his life to Wild Turkey.

Bottling that life-changing moment, Master Distiller Eddie Russell introduces an extraordinary bourbon made from his private selection of barrels in Rickhouse A. The marriage of these precious barrels laid to rest in the last 13 years results in a spectacular experience.

Layers of toffee and honey give way to fruity notes of candied pear, stewed apples, spice, subtle oak and vanilla, before delivering a long, lingering and caramel finish. To Eddie Russell, Master's Keep 1894 is perfection in a bottle—an ode to that dream-like summer day in historic Rickhouse A.

I've heard Eddie Russell share this recollection on more than one occasion. As I mentioned previously, it's a wonderful story, and I enjoy hearing it every time it's told. Naturally, a story of such importance should have a whiskey to carry its emotional weight, shouldn't it? I'm going to pause right there and move forward with the tasting. I have a lot to say about Master's Keep 1894, but I think it's best we gain perspective on the bourbon itself before continuing the discussion.

Wild Turkey
Master's Keep 1894

SPIRIT:	Kentucky straight bourbon whiskey
PROOF:	90
AGE:	not stated (reportedly six, eleven, and thirteen years)
MISC.:	bottled by Wild Turkey Distilling Co., Lawrenceburg, KY; batch #0001, bottle #05006
	tasted neat in a Glencairn Glass after a few minutes rest…
COLOR:	amber
NOSE:	vanilla, toffee, honey, orange zest, light oak, graham crackers, pastry dough, hints of roasted nuts
TASTE:	mild vanilla, toffee, Golden Delicious apples, baking spice, faint musty oak
FINISH:	medium-short—vanilla, toffee, light caramel, oak, brief peppery spice

OVERALL:

Well, that's disappointing. I'm sorry. I honestly don't like saying it's disappointing, but it's true. While Master's Keep 1894 isn't bad bourbon, it's not impressive bourbon either. The nose is light, the flavor is light, and the finish is light. It's Wild Turkey light. If there's thirteen-year bourbon in here, it's either from the lowest floors or significantly diluted. According to The Whisky Ledger (which asked Eddie directly), it's a blend of six-, eleven-, and thirteen-year bourbon from rickhouse A. Sounds like a rickhouse-limited Rare Breed diluted to 90 proof, and it very much tastes that way. Not at all what I was expecting for an exclusive release. I mean, I knew it was a lower-proof expression going into the tasting, but so are Diamond Anniversary and Master's Keep Seventeen-Year. Each of those limited editions are more complex and flavorful.

So, what's going on? How did this come to be? Why Australia only? And why the hefty price tag ($199 AUS)? I'll start by saying I don't have definitive answers. I want to make that crystal clear. I'll give you my best guesses  and develop from there. I'd ask Eddie directly, but I feel bad enough even typing this review (awful, actually). Wild Turkey is my passion. As much as I'd like to give nothing but glowing reviews and offer spin-positive criticism, I just can't. There are plenty of whiskey blogs and reviewers out there doing that already. I'm focused on one thing and that's Wild Turkey. While my loyalty is with the brand, that loyalty is trusted by my readers. If I'm dishonest with a review, my blog is essentially worthless. I sincerely hope that Eddie and the folks at Wild Turkey and Campari understand this. Tough love is still love.

Let's start with how this whiskey came to be and why Australia only, as I believe they go hand in hand. Alcohol tax in Australia is outrageous. If you think American taxes on spirits are bad, research what Aussies deal with (about $83 AUS per liter of pure alcohol). That's the main reason Wild Turkey 101 isn't a staple down there (it's considered super-premium). Instead, they have Wild Turkey 86.8 proof as a standard. The last time the United States saw 86.8 as a core expression was in the mid to late 1980s. I suppose the taxes on Master's Keep Decades (104 proof) negatively affected net profit when factored into the $199 AUS (tax-inclusive) retail price. As a result, I believe Campari resolved to customize the next Master's Keep to fit the Australian marketplace, and therefore, increase net profit. Enter Master's Keep 1894 at 90 proof.

Do I really think Eddie Russell believes 1894 to be "perfection in a bottle?" Nah, I think that's marketing chatter typical of the bourbon industry. It's my opinion that Eddie was working within a box. He had to come up with a low-proof bourbon special enough for an Australian limited edition. The unique barrels used for Master's Keep 17-Year were gone, so he worked with what was left (possibly a few select barrels from the lowest floors of rickhouse A). My guess is those weren't enough to reach projected yield. How does one solve that problem? Find barrels from other floors, barrels you can dilute enough to stay within the confines of the metaphorical box. At least, that's how I'm envisioning it.

And the story? The heartfelt biographical narrative helps to frame the release as worthy, and thereby justifies (or at least attempts to justify) the hefty $199 AUS price tag. While I hate even thinking that, it's the best rationale I've got. Maybe I'm wrong. Maybe the batch came first. Maybe Eddie came up with this lower-proof six-, eleven-, and thirteen-year blend out of the blue and decided it was destined for Australia. I just don't see that. To me, Eddie's profile is Russell's Reserve Single Barrel Bourbon, and Master's Keep 1894 is very far from it (in profile and price).

What frustrates me most about Master's Keep 1894 echoes back to my introduction. It's an amazing story, but in the end it's about business. It's about selling bourbon with a story. It's not my story, but it's a damn good one, and I can't help but feel it deserves a better whiskey. Just because the first straight-from-the-barrel sip came from rickhouse A, that doesn't mean you have to use barrels from rickhouse A to tell that story. You don't even have to create a batch that duplicates the profile (or the memory of the profile) of the same barrel. Accuracy and art don't always go well together. Take, for example, Kevin Costner's *Wyatt Earp*. While arguably the more historically accurate film in comparison to Kurt Russell's *Tombstone*, *Tombstone* is a grand-slam entertainment masterpiece. I mean, how many Doc Holliday lines can you recite from *Wyatt Earp*? You're a daisy if you think it's more than one.

So, what's going on? Where am I going with this? Well, Val Kilmer's Doc Holliday would call it a reckoning. I call it taking account of the situation and setting things right. I noticed that some of the promotional materials for Master's Keep 1894 state "the third release." So, either Australia's 1894 will remain uniquely out of sequence from domestic Master's Keep releases, or they're going to get skipped at some point. Needless to say, Master's Keep Revival is coming soon (per an Alcohol and Tobacco Tax and Trade Bureau filing). Revival is stated (or at least filed) as a twelve-year Wild Turkey bourbon, finished in Oloroso Sherry casks and bottled at 101 proof. Sounds awesome, right? Well, I think it's only fair, considering the price/profile conflict with 1894, for Australia to see this release. In addition, I think it would be a prudent gesture to offer a mail-in rebate to Australian consumers that purchase (or have already purchased) 1894. Hell, it could even be a coupon for a future Wild Turkey purchase of any kind. Just something to help level the price/profile seesaw I just experienced.

As for giving Eddie's story the proper whiskey (remember, we want *Tombstone* not *Wyatt Earp*), I have an idea (with all due respect and admiration towards Eddie). First off, let's consider 1894 a tribute to rickhouse A and leave it at that. Next, I'd kindly ask Eddie to open a bottle of 1981 Wild Turkey 101 (remember, '81 was the year he took that first straight-from-the-barrel sip). Study and savor it until that bottle is all you breathe and taste in your mind. Then, search every barrel of every floor of every rickhouse until you develop a batch that's nearly comparable (I get that '81 is Glut Era whiskey, but work with me here). When you're satisfied and confident this masterful batch is complete, name it Master's Keep 1981 and let that be your true "perfection in a bottle." I realize things have changed and the profile won't be the same, but I know for a fact it could get close. I've tasted some superb Russell's Reserve barrels; Eddie, you've tasted a thousand times more. Master's Keep 1981 . . . it's your huckleberry.

I should probably wrap things up. To my readers, I thank you for your patience, as this review has been considerably lengthier (my longest review to date by far). To Eddie Russell and the folks at Wild Turkey/Campari, I sincerely appreciate your attention and hope that you at least understand my point of view. You don't have to agree with it; I only ask that you take my words to heart. Master's Keep 1894 is, at best, a mid-shelf bourbon in top-tier packaging. If Master's Keep 17-Year and Decades were no longer available in Australia, then I might recommend 1894 as a gift for the diehard Wild Turkey fan that appreciates a substantially lighter (proof and flavor) bourbon. Outside of that, you're better off with a couple bottles of Wild Turkey 101. Simply put, the price/profile ratio is far too skewed to the left. While I'd love to give every Wild Turkey whiskey a solid gold five out of five, as Doc Holliday would say, my hypocrisy goes only so far.

The Best of 2017

Each December, "best of" whiskey posts flood social media and online publications. Many are mediocre, featuring the same old predictable labels year after year. Some are straight-up lame, offering little to no value for serious readers or experienced enthusiasts. A handful, I suspect, are influenced by cash and the desire to procure future whiskey releases and allocated rarities. Like it or not, my annual "best of" is all about Wild Turkey, and 2017 was my first. dj

DECEMBER 26, 2017

This year I'm starting a new tradition. I'm calling it "The Best of Wild Turkey." The premise is simple: select a few noteworthy releases from the past year to spotlight. While ratings will certainly factor into my selection process, they won't be the sole determining factor. The goal is to recognize Wild Turkey releases that aren't just quality pours but offer traits one could argue as special and worthy of one's attention.

My rules are straightforward. To be eligible for selection, a release must be all of the following:

1. Produced at Wild Turkey Distillery and bottled and/or initially available for sale within the same calendar year. That means no "dusties" or bottles from previous years.

2. Private single barrels, independent bottlings, and Campari Whiskey Baron releases are all potential selections (so long as they're confirmed as Wild Turkey produced).

3. While some whiskeys are eligible for multiple categories, each category will have an exclusive winner. In other words, you won't find a particular whiskey winning multiple categories.

So, without further delay, I present to you *Rare Bird 101*'s Best of Wild Turkey 2017.

BEST DESIGN (2017)

CAMPARI WHISKEY BARONS No. 1

(OLD RIPY AND BOND & LILLARD)

Sure, the initial Whiskey Barons series is pricey, limited in availability, and arguably disappointing when factoring flavor profiles into a quality/value ratio. They aren't bad whiskeys; they just fail to measure up to other less-expensive Wild Turkey and Russell's Reserve options. That being said, the designs of both Old Ripy and Bond & Lillard (glass and labels) are superb, each cleverly accomplishing the look of early twentieth-century medicinal whiskey pints, but doing so with sleek pop flair. Bravo, Campari design team!

Best Core Expression (2017)
Wild Turkey Rare Breed
(Batch 116.8)

After nearly three years of Rare Breed 112.8 (a notable step down from batch 03RB, in my opinion), Wild Turkey issued a new and improved Rare Breed batch, with a redesigned bottle and label to boot. Boasting an ABV of 58.4% (the highest-proof Rare Breed batch to date), Rare Breed 116.8 packs a punch in strength and flavor. Profile-wise, it's everything I love about modern Wild Turkey 101, albeit kicked up a notch.

While I long for a return of the mature Rare Breed profiles of old, based on the popularity of whiskey these days, it's probably not happening anytime soon. In the meantime, I'll happily take this step in the right direction. Nice work Jimmy and Eddie!

BEST STRAIGHT BOURBON (2017)
WILD TURKEY MASTER'S KEEP DECADES

After more than a year without a Wild Turkey limited edition, 2017 saw the return of Master's Keep. This time, instead of an age-stated offering, like 2015's Master's Keep 17-Year, a blend of several straight bourbons ranging in age from ten to twenty years were chosen. Bottled at 104 proof, non-chill filtered, and packaged in the same classy manner as the original Master's Keep, Decades had a lot going for it before it even hit retail shelves. It more than delivered. The rich vanilla, toffee, candy-like citrus, and a near-perfect sweet-musty oak presence showcases the best of both classic and modern Wild Turkey profiles. It's a fantastic pour and Eddie Russell deserves the credit. Well done, sir.

BEST STRAIGHT RYE (2017)
WILD TURKEY 101 RYE

I've been a fan of Wild Turkey 101 Rye for some time now. Sure, it's changed a little over the last ten years or so, but it's always an enjoyable pour and blows any other Kentucky straight rye whiskey in its price tier out of the water. When I learned from Bruce Russell that 2017's 101 Rye was produced at the new distillery, it made perfect sense.

This year's Wild Turkey 101 Rye is a notable step up in quality and complexity, and I find myself enjoying it regularly. If this is any sign of what's to come from future Wild Turkey rye expressions, then expect some amazing releases. Congratulations to Jimmy and Eddie for a successful transition to the new distillery. The proof is in this whiskey!

BEST SINGLE BARREL (2017)

WHISKY JEWBILEE
(WILD TURKEY #3426, J&J SPIRITS)

I'd been looking forward to the 2017 Chicago Whisky Jewbilee from the day I sampled the 2016 New York Jewbilee. Thankfully, 2017's Jewbilee did not disappoint. Thick molasses, vanilla bean, cherry pie filling, clove, cinnamon, leather . . . the notes (and warmth) go on and on with this one.

For those who haven't quite figured it out yet, barrel-proof, single-barrel Wild Turkey bourbon is extremely rare. Save for finding late-1990's "Donuts" on the secondary market, J&J Spirits Wild Turkey bottles are your only true shot at a purchase. That said, it's not just ABV and rarity that makes this bourbon special—it's a damn fine barrel, plain and simple. The 2017 Chicago Jewbilee is a testament to the quality of modern Wild Turkey and one more demonstration of Joshua Hatton and Jason Johnstone-Yellin's skill. Take a bow, fellas.

KENTUCKY STRAIGHT BOURBON WHISKEY

CASK NO. 3426
RICKHOUSE G. 6TH FLOOR
AGED 9 YEARS

Best Whiskey Overall (2017)

Russell's Reserve Single Barrel

(#16-490, Woodland Wine Merchant)

Let me start by saying I sipped a lot of Russell's Reserve Single Barrel bottlings this year. From standard releases to numerous private selections, I had a great time evaluating various nuanced profiles. But never have I experienced a profile quite like Woodland Wine Merchant's Russell's Reserve #16-490. While Davidson's #2394 was my long-standing favorite, the folks from Woodland Wine Merchant found a way to top it.

Russell's Reserve Single Barrel #16-490 is a well-aged colossus. Featuring rich, robust, and uniquely "woody" notes that one could argue are reminiscent of Wild Turkey from decades ago, this selection is a remarkable gem. It's a crying shame there were only forty-two bottles filled from this barrel, but perhaps that's the price paid for perfection. The angels may have taken their share, but what they left behind is glorious. Hats off to the folks at Woodland Wine for recognizing the beauty of barrel #16-490, *Rare Bird 101*'s Best Whiskey of 2017.

FROM GRAIN TO BOTTLE, DESIGN TO RETAIL (AND EVERYTHING IN BETWEEN), YOU ALL DESERVE A HUGE PAT ON THE BACK.

Thanks to everyone involved in the production, selection, and marketing of these award-winning whiskeys. From grain to bottle, design to retail (and everything in between), you all deserve a huge pat on the back. Here's to what 2018 may bring . . . cheers!

The New Golden Age of Wild Turkey (& Why You Should Be Paying Attention)

By the Spring of 2018, I had gained a better understanding of Wild Turkey's rich history. With changes in ownership, facilities, and flavor profiles over the last forty years, it seemed only appropriate to divide that timespan into specific eras. In the process, I came to the realization that today's Wild Turkey might just be the best Wild Turkey.

As it turns out, the piece caught the attention of Campari, and they requested permission to share it via Twitter. I'll never forget receiving that email, standing in the break room at work, coffee in one hand, cell phone in the other. I was elated. It was the first time Campari formally acknowledged my passion for their brand. I wasn't looking for praise or reward, but I was happy someone in an official capacity was reading my work. It felt like a huge personal victory. dj

For decades, Wild Turkey has suffered an undeserved rough reputation. Most companies would consider that a serious problem—one best addressed with careful PR and possible rebranding. I'm not sure how talks in the boardroom of Austin, Nichols & Co. went, or Pernod Ricard, or even Campari for that matter, but I can tell you how the Russells addressed it. Regardless of ownership, they kept making quality bourbon and rye whiskey and continue to do so to this day. Reputation be damned: they stay true to their craft, respect their consumers, and in all ways embrace the distinctive label that started it all.

Unlike many distilleries that simply hire and fire distillers as needed, Wild Turkey has a family legacy to pass on. It may not be family owned, but it's most certainly family operated. And let's be honest, when it comes to the Russells, nobody's sitting around. Jimmy could (and honestly deserves to) be living on beachfront property with his toes in the sand, but instead he gets up each morning and goes to work. Eddie carries the same work ethic and, in my opinion, is crafting bourbon that rivals some of Jimmy's finest. And now a third generation is learning the ropes. Brand Ambassador

THE TORCH IS PASSING HAND TO HAND, FATHER TO SON, AND THUS THE CRAFT STAYS TRUE.

Bruce Russell, who is currently based in Austin, TX, is spending more time in Lawrenceburg working directly with his father.

So, let's stop and take a look at where we're at today. There are now three generations of Russells, father to son, actively involved with the production of Kentucky straight bourbon whiskey for the same distillery. How often has that happened? Someone once joked that before Prohibition there were at least twelve Ripys making whiskey where Wild Turkey Distillery now stands. Of course, there's Beams and Noes. But three paternal generations at the same location producing the same bourbon whiskey together is a truly rare occurrence. The torch is passing hand to hand, father to son, and thus the craft stays true. And the timing couldn't be better, as I genuinely believe we've entered a New Golden Age of Wild Turkey.

THE GOLDEN AGE OF WILD TURKEY

How does one define a Golden Age? Some sources state a Golden Age is "a period of great happiness, prosperity, and achievement" (*Merriam-Webster*), while other sources describe it as "a period when a specified art, skill, or activity is at its peak" (*Oxford Lexico*). Let's take both definitions and apply them to Wild Turkey.

As much as enthusiasts love Glut Era Wild Turkey (about 1979–1991), it most certainly wasn't a prosperous time for the brand, or bourbon in general. One could argue there was achievement in navigating the storm. However, while commendable, survival isn't a trait of a golden age, so let's go ahead and scratch that era off the list. And while we're at it, let's take the Early Years (1942–1966) off the table as well. Most of this era's bourbon was sourced from various Kentucky distilleries, and the rye from Maryland and

Pennsylvania. While Wild Turkey was no doubt a successful and growing brand, I wouldn't consider that period a Golden Age by definition.

How about the years when Jimmy Russell first took the reins (1967–1978)? From all accounts, there was happiness, prosperity, and achievement. Jimmy was in his prime, and the bourbon whiskey being produced at that time is considered by many enthusiasts to be second to none. There was innovation with the creation of new expressions, like Wild Turkey Liqueur (now American Honey), as well as the introduction of collectible ceramic decanters. This period fits our definition and is unquestionably a top candidate for a Golden Age.

Now, let's take a look at the post-Glut Era (1992–1998), or what I consider a Turkey Renaissance. By this time, Eddie Russell had been on board for over a decade, though Jimmy was still very much in charge. The Glut Era was ending, and new products were coming out of the distillery nearly every other year. The 1990s saw the introduction of Rare Breed and Kentucky Spirit, as well as the continuance of Wild Turkey 101 12-Year with the "Split Label." Two of these products, Rare Breed and Kentucky Spirit, would eventually become core expressions. The export variety increased as well in the 1990s, with Wild Turkey Cuvee LaFayette, 1855 Reserve, Tradition, and the travel-retail Kentucky Legend. With so much moving in a positive direction, one might consider this the Golden Age. I don't think so, but keep reading and I'll offer my reasons later.

The years following the 1990s are what I think of as Transitional Years for Wild Turkey (1999–2006). Logos and core expression labels were redesigned after decades of use. The revered Wild Turkey 101 12-Year expression became export only. New products, like Russell's Reserve 10-Year, were introduced then quickly reintroduced at a lower proof. Rare Breed stopped becoming a uniquely proofed annual batch; bottling moved from Kentucky to Indiana, then later Indiana to Arkansas; barrel-entry proof changed, not once but twice; and product consistency was arguably askew. While there were notable releases throughout this period, there's

far too much change and apparent uncertainty to classify these years as "Golden" by any stretch of the definition.

I'll now use the word "modern" loosely as a descriptor used in relation to anything remotely in the present. It'll work for now, but some years down the road (should this article still exist), one should revise the discussion that follows appropriately.

Let's talk about modern Wild Turkey (2007–2014). I'll split this era into two periods: the Early Modern and the Late Modern. In general, the Early-Modern period is distinguished as the final years of ownership under Pernod Ricard (2007–2009). While new releases, like Russell's Reserve 6-Year Rye and limited editions like the fourteen-year Tradition, were trickling out, the overall Wild Turkey bourbon profile was beginning to change. Russell's Reserve 10-Year was no longer the dusty-esque 101/12-like pour it had been. Wild Turkey 101 was losing some of its classic "funkiness," as was Rare Breed. And Kentucky Spirit, while still an amazing single-barrel bourbon, wasn't exactly the same as its releases in the 1990s and early 2000s. The profile changes were likely a combination of many factors, but as for the overall business direction, I'm curious if Pernod Ricard assumed

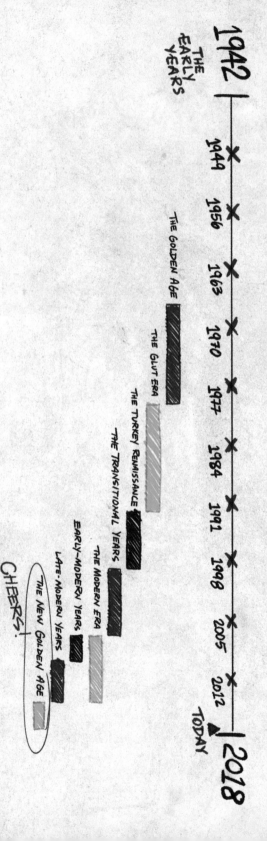

Wild Turkey Eras

1942 — THE EARLY YEARS

1944 ✕

1956 ✕

1963 ✕ — THE GOLDEN AGE

1970 ✕ — THE GLUT ERA

1977 ✕ — THE TURKEY RENAISSANCE

1984 ✕ — THE TRANSITIONAL YEARS

1991 ✕ — THE MODERN ERA

1998 ✕ — EARLY-MODERN YEARS

2005 ✕ — LATE-MODERN YEARS

2012 ✕ — THE NEW GOLDEN AGE · CHEERS!

TODAY ▲

2018

what was coming and simply started coasting. Regardless, by mid-2009, Gruppo Campari had taken over, and despite what anyone tells you, it was a good thing for Wild Turkey.

The Late-Modern period (2010–2014) saw new life breathed into Wild Turkey thanks to focused creative efforts by both Campari and the Russells. In fact, the wheels started turning in a very short time. By 2011, a new state-of-the-art distillery was fully operational, and revised logos and labels for several core expressions started rolling out. In 2013, Russell's Reserve Single Barrel Bourbon debuted, followed closely by a private barrel selection program. The year 2014 saw two major events: the grand opening of a new Wild Turkey Visitor Center and Jimmy Russell's sixtieth anniversary (marked by a special bourbon release, of course). Overall, the Late-Modern period brought quick change—positive change—and the stage was set for what I believe are the best years Wild Turkey would see in decades.

Before I discuss the times we're living in now, I want to circle back and nail down my definitive Golden Age of Wild Turkey. For me that would be the pre-Glut years, when Jimmy was first designated as Master Distiller (1967–1978). Yes, the post-Glut 1990s, or what I call the Turkey Renaissance, is a potential candidate for a golden age; the problem is, things were still shaky coming out of the Glut Era. The venerable eight-year age statement for Wild Turkey 101 was dropped domestically in exchange for the infamous "Old No.8" label, and exports were seemingly getting more attention. It just can't compare to the late '60s and early '70s, when Austin, Nichols realized what Jimmy was doing in Lawrenceburg was magical. So much so, they purchased the distillery itself, establishing it as the only source for Wild Turkey bourbon and, eventually, rye whiskey. Those few years, and the years just prior to the Glut Era, were surely the definitive Golden Age of Wild Turkey.

The *New* Golden Age of Wild Turkey

Looking back on the last three years, I have to admit Wild Turkey is performing incredibly well (and I'm not just talking financially). While prosperous and contributing to the overall growth of the Campari family of brands, Wild Turkey is much larger than that. The creativity, craft, dedication—and most importantly the attitude—is unrivaled at its present level by any other Kentucky distillery. Everything seems to be moving in the right direction, with the right timing and the promise of better things to come.

Let's start by looking back at 2015. First and foremost, Eddie Russell was officially named Master Distiller. It was a title well-earned after many years of service under his father, Jimmy. And in case you haven't figured it out by now, Jimmy's not stepping down anytime soon. Speaking of the Russells, 2015 saw the addition of Eddie's son Bruce as a brand ambassador. Outside of personnel changes, the logos and labels for a vast majority of the core expressions were completely redesigned. As for new releases, there were two limited editions (Master's Keep 17-Year and Russell's Reserve 1998), as well as a new ultra-premium core expression, Russell's Reserve Single Barrel Rye. Each of these releases were well-received. In fact, many enthusiasts regard Russell's Reserve 1998 as one of the greatest Wild Turkey expressions ever bottled.

By 2016, Wild Turkey had gathered considerable steam. The private barrel selection program was growing increasingly popular among vendors and enthusiasts. Whiskey consumers who traditionally passed on the brand's offerings were taking note and branching out. And then, just when you thought things might be settling down, actor Matthew McConaughey was welcomed to the Wild Turkey family as Creative Director. This was no run-of-the-mill spokesperson's job. From the release of his first promotional video, it was apparent the relationship was the start of something far greater—something genuine and unique.

The New Golden Age of Wild Turkey

In the blink of an eye 2017 was here, and it brought with it two memorable releases: Master's Keep Decades and a new Rare Breed batch (116.8). Decades may be the most artfully crafted limited-edition whiskey ever released by Wild Turkey. Sure, it's hard to measure up to fan favorites like Tribute and American Spirit, but that's not what I'm saying. What makes Decades so special is that it's a "concept album bourbon." Eddie skillfully married his own profile preferences and Jimmy's profile preferences into a single bourbon aged ten to twenty years. And it works . . . beautifully. It's small-batch blending at its finest and evidence that all the years—yes, decades—of tutelage under Jimmy paid off. In essence, Decades is the real Wild Turkey Tribute, and I think a lot of folks missed that subtlety.

As for 2017's Rare Breed, fans disappointed in batch 112.8 (raises hand) were treated to a notable step up in quality, as well as a new bottle and label design with batch 116.8. And Rare Breed wasn't the only expression experiencing an uptick in profile complexity. Both Wild Turkey 101 and Wild Turkey 101 Rye were each consistently impressive by the batch. Perhaps the six-year whiskey distilled at the new facility in 2011 was finally strutting its stuff? Hard to say, but something was definitely clicking in 2017.

And here we are in 2018. Longbranch, Matthew McConaughey and Eddie Russell's highly anticipated Wild Turkey collaboration, launched just days ago. It may not be every diehard bourbon enthusiast's dream release, but I imagine it's going to give its competition, like Basil Hayden's and Gentleman Jack, one hell of a Texas-sized bullfight. Time will tell, but my bet's on Longbranch. As for what else is to come, there's Master's Keep Revival and Russell's Reserve 2002. Revival is essentially Wild Turkey 101 12-Year finished in Oloroso sherry barrels (yes, that sounds delicious). Russell's Reserve 2002 appears to be the sequel to Russell's Reserve 1998. If it's anything near 1998 in profile, get ready for a stellar straight bourbon whiskey!

Folks, we are without question living in a New Golden Age of Wild Turkey. Enthusiasts exploring the brand have more variety to choose from than any generation before it. There's truly something for everyone. As for you old-school enthusiasts stuck on dusty expressions, take a minute to put the "forward-facing turkey" bottle back in the cabinet. Drive to your local and pick-up a Russell's Reserve Single Barrel private selection. Take a chance on Decades or the seventeen-year Master's Keep (if you can find them). Hell, grab a new bottle of Wild Turkey 101 or 101 Rye and pop the cork with an open mind. Yes, dusty Turkey is phenomenal, but it's a dying breed. Give today's Wild Turkey a fair chance, and I'm confident that everything I'm saying will make perfect sense in a rather short time.

As for the future, we have a lot to look forward to in both the short and long term. From a reported 101st anniversary release celebrating the combined years of service of Jimmy and Eddie Russell, to rumors of a possible collectible decanter, there's more on the way. We also get to find out how well-aged whiskey from the new distillery performs, and that's something a whiskey nerd like me lives for.

Looking further down the road, Bruce Russell may just be the next Master Distiller of Wild Turkey. He comes from a different generation and is open to experimentation and modern trends. At the same time, he's cut from the same cloth as his father and grandfather. Bruce understands the foundation of his brand: the hardworking customers buying handles of Wild Turkey 101 every other week. From all I've seen, he seems to have an excellent understanding of what makes Wild Turkey, well, Wild Turkey, and that's something you can't create artificially.

Yes, I'd say Wild Turkey is in good hands, as it has been since 1954 when Jimmy first started. Oh, and as for the rough reputation that has endured so long . . . I say give it the bird! At the rate things are going, it's finally looking like Wild Turkey will have the last laugh.

WILD TURKEY MASTER'S KEEP REVIVAL

Wild Turkey Master's Keep Revival

After struggling with 2017's Master's Keep 1894,
Revival proved a refreshing joy to review. Two months
after posting, I met Eddie Russell in Columbia, South
Carolina, to select a Russell's Reserve Single Barrel
Bourbon for a local vendor. The conversation turned to
Revival, and he revealed some enlightening behind-the-
scenes details about its production process. We tasted
barrel-proof samples and sipped a 1990 "Cheesy Gold
Foil" Wild Turkey 101 12-Year, but Eddie's Revival story
was my favorite part of that summer afternoon. dj

JUNE 12, 2018

Looking back over the last three years at the Master's Keep series, there have been ups and downs; two hits and a single export-only miss (1894). Some enthusiasts have appreciated the series more than others, but as a whole, I consider it a successful run. Truth be told, we owe it all to Eddie Russell. While Jimmy will always be a legend among legends, Eddie has more than proven his worth as a master distiller. From Russell's Reserve Single Barrel (bourbon and rye), to an incredibly popular private barrel program, the Master's Keep releases are icing on an already impressive cake. And the latest in the Master's Keep lineup, Revival, is arguably one for the bourbon history books.

In 2004, Wild Turkey released Sherry Signature, a ten-year, 86-proof bourbon finished in Oloroso Sherry casks and "enhanced" with Oloroso Sherry as well. I'm not certain what "enhanced" means entirely, but I'm guessing a small amount of sherry wine was added to each batch. It was an export-only release, which saw considerable distribution in Europe (likely based on the popularity of sherry-finished Scotch). I've yet to taste Sherry Signature, but it obviously made an impression on Eddie Russell, as recalled on the liner notes of Revival's box:

> *Master's Keep Revival is the whiskey that Master Distiller Eddie Russell has dreamed of for decades. Years ago, Eddie's legendary father, Master Distiller Jimmy Russell, crafted an experimental bourbon enhanced with Oloroso Sherry that faded from existence but not from Eddie's mind. Now Eddie presents a stunning revival of that special bourbon—a mouthwatering memory, perfected and bottled.*
>
> *For 12 to 15 years, the bourbon in this limited edition rested in a reserved lot of American Oak Barrels before finishing in 20-year-old Spanish Oloroso Sherry casks that Eddie personally hand-selected during his travels to the Jerez-Xeres-Sherry region in Spain. The final result is an indulgent sipping whiskey with the warm and round characteristics of the Spanish Sherry, anchored perfectly by the backbone of a beautifully crafted bourbon.*

While some may be surprised that Eddie would take on a sherry-finished whiskey, it doesn't surprise me at all. From the moment Eddie began playing a larger role at Wild Turkey, he made it very clear that his tastes weren't necessarily Jimmy's. Eddie has long been an advocate of experimentation (within reason). We've seen it twice already: Forgiven, while not a personal favorite, is one such example, and more recently, Longbranch offered a new spin on traditional Wild Turkey bourbon. Again, not a personal favorite, but I appreciate his willingness to try different things. That takes skill and, arguably, courage. After all, in the case of Revival, you're risking choice

well-aged stocks and an investment in Spanish ex-sherry casks (which can't be cheap to import). Messing up isn't really an option.

Before I get to the tasting, I'd like to briefly remark on the packaging. Even though Revival shares the same basic box and bottle design as the other Master's Keep releases, the red faux-woodgrain box really catches the eye; it draws you in and looks fantastic on display. The burgundy neck strip adds a classy touch, as does the name itself . . . Revival. It's a fitting title for the domestic return of Wild Turkey 101 12-Year, as well as the rebirth of a mid-2000's sought-after rarity. It's an enticing presentation that, in some ways, helps one justify paying the ultra-premium price ($150 SRP).

As I pour this whiskey, I can't help but feel a bit nervous for Eddie. With so many Wild Turkey fans awaiting the return of a 101/12 expression, bringing it back as a finished offering could very well backfire. Not everyone is a fan of finished American whiskeys, and the traditional Wild Turkey fan base isn't typically an experiment-loving bunch. Rather, they're hardworking folks who appreciate a quality pour at a reasonable price. Paying for an expensive Wild Turkey expression for special occasions is one thing, but taking that risk on an experimental version is another. But here's the good news: I know how this story ends.

Those familiar with my reviews know that just because I write in present tense, doesn't mean I haven't spent plenty of time with a pour beforehand.

In fact, my Patreon supporters get early insight into all my first pours—this one was particularly fun to share last week. Special thanks to Ryan Alves for posting his thoughts on Revival as well, especially the nod to his grandfather. It's a beautiful thing when a whiskey transports you back in time to a memory or remembrance of a loved one. At that point, it transcends ratings and criticism. It's what a master distiller likely wants most: a whiskey you'll cherish for reasons beyond taste alone.

I have a lot to say about Revival but few things as important as that last sentence. I'll enjoy this pour and try to give you an idea of what you'll experience, but needless to say, it's something far greater than tasting notes or critical impressions.

Wild Turkey Master's Keep Revival

SPIRIT: Kentucky straight bourbon whiskey finished in Oloroso Sherry casks

PROOF: 101

AGE: twelve years

MISC.: bottled by Wild Turkey Distilling Co., Lawrenceburg, KY; batch #0001, bottle #28162

tasted neat in a Glencairn Glass after a few minutes rest…

COLOR: rose copper

NOSE: (captivating, unique) plum, antique leather, caramel drizzle, charred oak, cinnamon-raisin bread, brown sugar, tobacco, hints of raspberries and herbs

TASTE: (silky mouthfeel) sherry, leather, sun-dried oak, caramel, fig, roman nougat, plum, black walnut, light baking spice, faint smoke

FINISH: long and lingering—"sherry-vanilla," chocolate-covered raisins, leather, semi-sweet oak, molasses, clove, hints of pecan shell and black pepper

OVERALL:

There is beauty in this glass. Marvelous, really. Master's Keep Revival is hands down the best sherry-finished straight bourbon whiskey I've ever tasted, and I don't mean that lightly. Throughout each phase of tasting, this whiskey excels at intricacy and balance. From an enchanting nose to a lingering finish, each breath, sip, and exhale is cause for pause. Whereas many whiskeys (particularly bourbons) tend to follow what I call the "A, B, C" pattern (nose, taste, finish), with each subsequent phase a step down in complexity, Revival is undoubtedly "A, A, A." And while the Oloroso influence is clearly notable, it's certainly not overdone. Honestly, it's perfect. Not only did Eddie Russell select bourbons with suitable maturation, he knew precisely how long they needed to rest in finishing casks.

When I reviewed Master's Keep 1894 last year, I discussed storytelling and how it's commonplace in American whiskey—particularly when it comes to marketing limited editions. It's not uncommon for producers to incorporate a story into a release, yet far too often these tales, and the whiskeys they're associated with, fall flat. Unsurprisingly, the very method used to increase expectations is the primary reason they fail (as expectations simply aren't met). Fortunately, Master's Keep Revival doesn't need a story to give it purpose. Sure, we read about Eddie's travels in Spain and his selection of twenty-year-old Jerez-Xeres-Sherry regional casks. But that's not a tale; that's a business trip. Revival doesn't need a backstory—Revival tells its own story.

Very rarely does a whiskey accomplish what Master's Keep Revival has. There's complexity in its uniqueness and completeness, yet elusiveness in exactly what makes those traits so gratifying. It has intrigue, mystery, revelation, wonder, and closure. It reminds you of the past, opens your mind to the future, and ultimately provides a sipping experience that very few American whiskeys can (or ever do). Last year, Master's Keep Decades received praise from numerous critics and industry publications, ranking third overall in *Whisky Advocate's* Best of 2017. With Revival, Wild Turkey has an even stronger contender for 2018's Whisky of the Year.

Well done, Mr. Russell. Revival is truly a masterwork.

Russell's Reserve Single Barrel:
Master Distiller Selection
2018 & "Noe Mercy"

As much as I enjoy writing, I've never been one to pen fiction. This post is an exception.

For some reason, be it my fascination with a barrel selection involving four acclaimed Kentucky master distillers, or a recently completed binge-watch of HBO's *Game of Thrones*, it just so happened I steered that fateful August day in the direction of pure fantasy. dj

AUGUST 21, 2018

When successful musicians get together, they call it a supergroup. When superheroes join together, they call it a super team. When Kentucky master distillers get together, they call it . . . well, a bunch of country boys sipping bourbon whiskey, of course. They may not sing like the Highwaymen or fight like the Avengers, but I guarantee they always have one hell of a good time.

A few weeks ago, a curious new Russell's Reserve Single Barrel Bourbon showed up in the Wild Turkey Visitor Center, simply labeled "Master Distiller Selection 2018," with no other description or display to explain exactly what those words meant. Was it a Jimmy pick? An Eddie pick? A Jimmy and Eddie pick? No one really knew. Thankfully, an incredible Turkey friend gave me a heads up, and I was able to purchase a bottle before they sold out.

With this new Russell's Reserve Single Barrel in hand, I decided I'd take on some detective work of my own. I reached out to Eddie Russell to find out its origin, and he quickly informed me that it was selected by himself, Jimmy, Fred Noe of Jim Beam, and Chris Morris of Woodford Reserve at the time of the 2018 Kentucky Bourbon Affair tasting. You read that correctly: four world-class Kentucky bourbon whiskey master distillers selecting a Wild Turkey barrel. When I read those names on my cell phone, my jaw dropped. This was indeed a special bottle. Naturally, my mind raced at the thought of those esteemed gentlemen, all at one table, enjoying the best of House Russell.

I'm not privy to the actual details of that epic gathering or how many barrels were tasted or selected, but that doesn't mean I can't share my version of the events—at least my "based on a true story" version. I thought today's review would be an excellent time to share it. So, pour your favorite Russell's Reserve Single Barrel selection, sit back, and let your mind drift away to the blue hills of Kentucky . . .

"Noe Mercy"

It was a pleasant spring day in Lawrenceburg. With a copper thief in his left hand and a copita in his right, Eddie Russell took the short walk to rickhouse B. His goal was simple: find a set of impressive Wild Turkey barrels for the 2018 Kentucky Bourbon Affair Master Distillers Tasting. Jimmy didn't accompany Eddie on this walk—didn't need to. He'd trained Eddie well. Indeed, the once Bourbon Apprentice was now an experienced Bourbon Master.

It's unknown exactly how much time Eddie spent in rickhouse B. Some say minutes, others say hours, but every eyewitness agrees on one thing: when Eddie strolled out, his smile was ten miles wide.

Eddie's next stop was rickhouse G. It was a straightforward visit. There was a barrel he'd hidden from Jamie Farris some months back, and today was the day to claim it. In, out, done.

Jimmy sat quietly with a stern innocence, while Eddie casually chatted and remarked on the barrel's details here and there.

With B and G selections behind him, there was one barrel left to find. As Eddie headed back towards the distillery, the setting sun cast a glorious light on rickhouse D. It was then Eddie scrapped his original plan of pulling a barrel from the famed rickhouse A, and instead made his way into D.

Some time passed, it grew dark, and Eddie had yet to exit. But just as workers began to grow concerned, a maniacal laughter echoed through the rickhouse. While some are certain it was Eddie's, others swear they heard cell phone speaker chatter and a slightly distorted, "Alright, alright, alright."

Weeks rolled by, and the day of the KBA Master Distillers Tasting finally arrived. Jimmy and Eddie each took a seat at the tasting room table and waited patiently for their special guests. Woodford Reserve's Chris Morris was first to walk through the door. Beaming with confidence and pride, Chris shook hands with the Russells and took his seat next to Eddie. A few short minutes later, Jim Beam's Fred Noe entered the room. Following immediately behind was Bruce Russell, who'd started up a friendly chat with Fred in the hall. With pleasantries and a few laughs exchanged by all, Fred took a seat next to Jimmy. The room grew eerily quiet as Bruce made his exit, slowly closing the door behind him. And just as the door was nearly shut, a strange music resonated from the hallway . . . an odd melody . . . medieval, even. While unconfirmed, I've been told that Bruce's ringtone was at one time "The Rains of Castamere." Something was most certainly afoot.

And so, the tasting began. First it was the rickhouse B barrel. Jimmy sat quietly with a stern innocence, while Eddie casually chatted and remarked on the barrel's details here and there. It was the honey barrel of honey barrels, and the Russells played their hand like Rainman at a novice dealer's table.

The sweat beaded on Chris's forehead, Fred started on a throat-clearing fit that came and went like a train on shaky tracks, and Jimmy just sat quietly smiling on the inside. Not wanting their nerves to show, both Chris and Fred offered a few conservative compliments about the selection. It was too good—unbelievably good—and something had to give. Luckily, there were two barrels left. An escape seemed almost easy.

The rickhouse G barrel was next. "Oh, damn," thought Fred. It was an incredible pour, possibly better than the rickhouse B barrel. Things were getting real serious, real quick.

And that's about when Chris spoke up. "Hey, um . . . so, I think . . ." His words trailed off as he fumbled around for his water bottle. After a swig that seemed to last five minutes, Chris finished his sentence. "So, yeah . . . I think this one's a little too mature. Got any younger barrels we could try?"

Fred jumped in. "Yeah, I agree. I think we should try something . . . with maybe lighter vanilla and some peanut notes. Something like that. Or wait . . . I heard those J&J guys found a great reject barrel. Got any rejects we can taste?" At this point, Fred's brow line was showing as much sweat as Chris's, and the formerly stealthy handkerchief dabs were now obvious displays of perspiration control.

Jimmy motioned to Eddie, and Eddie reached for the last bottle. "Fellas," said Eddie, "I'm sorry, but we've only got one sample left." It was taking everything Eddie had in him not to crack a guilty smile. He pictured a celebratory aftermath in his head . . . Jimmy's chuckles, high fives with Bruce,

McConaughey playing bongos . . . it was all happening. Then Eddie caught Jimmy's eye; his silent message delivered with a marksman's accuracy. The deed was unfinished, and Eddie needed to keep it together.

The last glasses were filled and, at this point, all Chris and Fred could do was pray for a miracle. Alas, it would never come. House Russell had delivered the final blow, and it came from rickhouse D. The boys from Woodford and Beam surrendered to the fact that Wild Turkey had something far too special to run from. They each mustered smiles and made their best attempts to appear as if they were at least mulling over a decision. In reality, Chris was trying to remember his most recent retirement account balance—would it be enough? Fred, on the other hand, contemplated an extended TV contract and raise for Mila Kunis.

Out of the foggy silence Jimmy spoke up: "I think that's it, boys. Whatcha got in mind?" Jimmy gently tapped the table, adding just the right amount of tension as Chris and Fred finally caved. Like insects fatigued in a spider's web, they were done.

Chris was the first to speak. "I guess . . . just whatever that last one was."

Then Fred responded, "Yeah, it was . . . nice. Fine, really. D was that it? D? Okay, yeah."

Jimmy and Eddie looked at each other, then Eddie replied, "D it is. Thanks for coming fellas! I'll show you out." And with that Eddie opened the tasting room door.

Fred Noe was the first to leave. If you've ever seen the movie *Shane*, that's how Fred rode off. Was he wounded or just tired? I guess we'll never know for sure.

Chris Morris, still seated at the table, had a look of disbelief behind a fragile smile. "What just happened?" he asked himself. At that very moment, he felt a pat on his shoulder. Chris turned around to find a grinning Jimmy Russell standing behind him.

"That's what we call Wild Turkey," said Jimmy. He gave Chris's shoulder one last pat, turned around, chuckled, and walked out the door.

Eddie led Chris out of the room and down the hallway. "Thanks again," said Eddie.

Chris, still stunned, nodded, and waved as he walked out the building.

It was over. Eddie headed back to the tasting room and gathered up the sample bottles. He took one last sip of the D barrel, smiled, and pulled out his cell phone. It was bongo time.

Alright, so that may not be exactly how it happened, but like I said before, "based on a true story."

At the end of the day, all that really matters is the whiskey in the bottle. Details are fun and frequently offer perspective (a point of profile reference, if you will), but it's the bourbon itself that matters most. So, without further fable or delay, let's give this Master Distiller Selection a healthy pour!

Russell's Reserve
Single Barrel Bourbon –
Master Distiller Selection 2018

SPIRIT: Kentucky straight bourbon whiskey

PROOF: 110

AGE: not stated

MISC.: barrel #17-781, rickhouse D, floor six; distilled and bottled by the
Wild Turkey Distilling Co., Lawrenceburg, KY
tasted neat in a Glencairn Glass after a few minutes rest…

COLOR: deep copper

NOSE: (robust and bakery sweet) brown sugar, toasted caramel,
molasses, charred honey-oak, maple syrup, vanilla bean, nutmeg,
cinnamon sticks, orange peel, herbal spice, leather, hints of clove
tobacco and chocolate-covered cherries

TASTE: (creamy and rich) caramel chews, vanilla spice, sweet hearty-oak,
brown sugar, dense honey-maple, nutmeg, buttered cinnamon
rolls, blood orange, herbal tea and leather

FINISH: long and flavorful—rich vanilla, caramel, charred oak, maple
syrup, brown sugar, crème brûlée, sweet herbal spice, cinnamon,
nutmeg, hints of leather and pepper

OVERALL:

Regardless of who selected this barrel (it all starts with a Russell), there's one
thing I know for sure… it's seriously delicious bourbon. Rich, robust, creamy, and
unmistakably Wild Turkey, this bottle has arguably everything you could want in
a modern release. In many ways, it reminds me of another stellar Russell's Reserve
Single Barrel private selection: Motor Supply Company's 2018 rickhouse D #17-
814. Between the two, I'll have to give the edge to this Master Distiller Selection.
There's just something about its slightly darker nose, its faintly earthy finish.
There's a subtle intensity that immediately draws you in, begging contemplation
but never once demanding it.

Did I just get lucky? Did I just happen to run across the best of the lot? I don't think do. All I can say is I've rarely been so impressed. Some people give sole credit to the individuals participating in selections. Personally, I think that's a little pretentious. Eddie humbly gives credit to time and Mother Nature. When it comes to quality Wild Turkey single barrels, I think the majority credit is always due the Russells, and I'd like to believe that Fred Noe, Chris Morris, and any other master distiller would agree.

Folks, I've said it before, and I'll say it again: 2018 is the year for Russell's Reserve private selections. So many excellent ones to choose from; so little time and resources to find them all. If you're not out there trying and buying these, you're honestly missing out.

DID I JUST GET LUCKY? I DON'T THINK SO.

HACKING
WILD TURKEY

Hacking Wild Turkey

In 2017, Aaron Goldfarb penned the article "How Wild Turkey 'Funk' Became a Whiskey Geek Obsession" for the online magazine *PUNCH*. I was interviewed for the piece, which led to an unexpected influx of traffic to my blog. Looking back, it was the push I needed.

The following year, Aaron authored *Hacking Whiskey: Smoking, Blending, Fat Washing, and Other Whiskey Experiments*, an adventurous book loaded with off-the-wall recipes, DIY blends, and crazy booze concoctions you'd never imagine. Two of my Wild Turkey blends were featured. Once again, I was grateful and thrilled to be included in Aaron's work. dj

SEPTEMBER 11, 2018

I'm willing to bet that most of you reading have, on more than one occasion, taken two or more straight whiskeys and blended them together. Sometimes the results were pleasing and sometimes the results were lacking, right? It ultimately came down to what your goals were and which whiskeys you elected to get there. Well, that's the focus of today's post—blending straight whiskeys, or more specifically, blending Wild Turkey straight whiskeys.

Unless you're new to whiskey enthusiasm, you've likely heard of infinity bottles, campfire whiskeys, and "Poor Man's Pappy." These, and many similar projects, are the subject of *Hacking Whiskey: Smoking, Blending, Fat Washing, and Other Whiskey Experiments*, the latest publication by author and friend Aaron Goldfarb,

If you like whiskey books about historical, initial-laden names, nineteenth-century liquor laws (yawn), bourbon fables, and distillery folklore, this isn't one of them. *Hacking Whiskey* is about having fun and getting crazy with whiskey. And nestled within its covers are two Wild Turkey blends from yours truly (thanks, Aaron). Since today's post is all about blends, I thought it would be a good idea to kick things off with a blend from the book.

WE WANT THE FUNK

Hang around bourbon enthusiasts long enough and you'll find the f-word frequently associated with Wild Turkey. F-U-N-K. Who doesn't want it? Well, probably Jimmy Russell. I've heard he's not fond of the phrase "Wild Turkey Funk." Nevertheless, it exists.

From my own experience, there isn't a single definitive "funk" note in Wild Turkey. That's why you typically don't find me referencing it in reviews nowadays. Generally speaking, I think "funk" relates to a variety of profiles. Obviously, there's dusty-era Turkey, with its intense herbal/floral perfume and dense musty oak. That's easily defined as funk in my opinion. Then we have what I consider the classic profile: rich honey-maple, herbal spice, and sweet musty oak. Funky? For some, sure—especially those more familiar with modern Wild Turkey. And finally, there's modern Wild Turkey with its nutty toffee and unique baking spice profile. I wouldn't necessarily define it "funky," but I certainly found it special when I first began appreciating it years ago. And about that time, I crafted the following recipe, which can be found in *Hacking Whiskey* (page 43).

* 65% Russell's Reserve Single Barrel Bourbon (110 proof; NAS, reportedly eight to ten years)
* 35% Wild Turkey Master's Keep (86.8 proof; seventeen years)

Net proof = 102 (approx.)

This was my first Wild Turkey blend I'd call a success. It was a naive attempt at recreating dusty Turkey magic; however, keep in mind that Master's Keep 17-Year was distilled in the late 1990s, and the Russell's Reserve Single Barrel Bourbon I used originally (a 2013 bottle) was distilled in the early to mid 2000s. While Master's Keep 17-Year was undoubtedly barreled at the old 107 barrel-entry proof, the 2013 Russell's Reserve Single Barrel may have been barreled at either 107 or 110 proof. (Still lower than the 115 barrel-entry proof used since 2006.) While barrel-entry proof is only one of many factors contributing to the dusty Turkey profile, it's a significant factor. That being said, if you try this blend, I'd recommend finding an older label Russell's Reserve Single Barrel or a modern private barrel selection showcasing classic Turkey character. You might just get lucky and capture some funky magic!

FORGIVEN BUT NOT FORGOTTEN

While I'm not a huge Wild Turkey Forgiven fan, a lot of folks out there are. Since it's very unlikely we'll see Forgiven return (at least in past form), I thought I'd give an honest shot at trying to hack it.

Truth be told, I've tried several custom Wild Turkey rye and bourbon blends. They've never really worked out for me. Maybe rye and bourbon blends just aren't my thing. When I want a rye, I sip a rye. When I want a bourbon, I sip a bourbon. I've never really needed a middle ground, though there's nothing wrong with preferring it. You like what you like.

Knowing that Forgiven contains younger whiskey bottled at 91 proof, I set off for my local to pick up an 81-proof Wild Turkey Bourbon. When I first popped the cork, I poured a few ounces for my 50/50 bourbon and Worcestershire burger marinade (simple yet awesome). After some tasty burgers and hot dogs, I immediately got to work. Following several attempts at different percentages, I finally nailed down a blend I feel matches Forgiven batch 303—at least as close as it's probably going to get with whiskeys that you'll find on a retail shelf.

* 50% Wild Turkey Bourbon (81 proof; NAS, "up to five to eight years")
* 40% Wild Turkey 101 Rye (101 proof; NAS, reportedly four to six years)
* 10% Wild Turkey 101 (101 proof; NAS, reportedly six to eight years)

Net proof = 91

And that's it. If you have Forgiven batch 303 on hand, give this blend a try. I wager you'll find the profiles are comparable. Interestingly, the proofs line up perfectly. Overall, it's about as close as you can get without hunting the real deal. But please don't take my word for it. Give it a shot and let me know what you think!

RARE BIRD 101

And last but certainly not least, my favorite Wild Turkey blend to date . . . Rare Bird 101. What is Rare Bird 101 (the blend)? I know, it's starting to sound like merchandise from *Spaceballs: The Movie*. But even so, I think Mel Brooks' Yogurt would approve.

In a nutshell, Rare Bird 101 is my own little recipe for making a more complex and developed Wild Turkey 101. Not that there's anything wrong with modern Wild Turkey 101. Not at all. I'm simply offering an alternative that hearkens back to days past yet maintains the essence of modern Wild Turkey in the process. You might call it "Decades Jr."

* 50% Wild Turkey Rare Breed 116.8 Proof (NAS, reportedly a batch of six-, eight-, and twelve-year bourbon)
* 25% Russell's Reserve 10 Year Old Bourbon (90 proof)
* 25% Wild Turkey Master's Keep (86.8 proof; seventeen years)*

Net proof = 102 (approx.)

This recipe is rather straightforward. Simple parts mean you don't have to turn your kitchen into Mr. Wizard's World. Use a shot glass for measuring or simply "eyeball it" in an everyday rocks glass. Give it a swirl and done. I think you'll discover this blend firmly rooted in the familiar Wild Turkey 101 profile, though laced with maturity and added complexity. The Rare Breed gives the blend a bold base, the Russell's Reserve 10-Year achieves dilution while introducing maturity at the same time, and the seventeen-year Master's Keep adds significant complexity from an era long gone. The combination of these three whiskeys makes for a near-101-proof bourbon you're sure to appreciate.

*Substitution: If you don't have Master's Keep 17-Year, try Master's Keep Decades. It will result in a slightly different profile, though arguably as delicious. In order to reach 101 proof, however, you'll need to add a little less Rare Breed (as Decades is 104 proof vs. the seventeen-year Master's Keep's 86.8 proof).

In closing, the main thing to remember when blending whiskey (Wild Turkey or otherwise) is to have fun. Try to have a goal in mind but don't get too disappointed if things turn out differently than you imagined. Sometimes surprises make for wonderful discoveries. Besides, whatever the outcome, you'll probably learn something new in the process, perhaps which profiles do or don't work well together and what's better left alone. At the end of the day, it all comes down to enjoying what's in your glass. If you accomplish that task . . . well, I'd call that success.

MY TURKEY HACK

_____
_____
_____
_____
_____
_____
_____
_____
_____
_____
_____
_____
_____
_____
_____
_____
_____
_____
_____

1972 Wild Turkey 101 & The Significance of Jimmy Russell

There are several individuals who keep my various projects going; T.J. Thompson is one of them. Since 2018, Grape & Grain Designs (formerly Thompson Woodworks) has provided unique handcrafted rewards for my patrons and supporters. He also shared a sizable pour of a 1972 Wild Turkey 101, which served as the backbone for this 2018 article-review combo. Thank you, T.J.

1970's Wild Turkey is a genuine rarity. While plenty was produced, plenty was consumed. Finding a bottle is an uncommon occurrence—finding a pristine bottle, even more so. If ever the opportunity to taste 1970s-era Wild Turkey comes your way, please take your time. Consider the circumstances surrounding its production, journal your thoughts, and without fail, offer a toast to the great Jimmy Russell. dj

OCTOBER 30, 2018

1972 was an important year for Wild Turkey. It was the first full year of ownership under Austin, Nichols & Co., who purchased the J.T.S. Brown & Sons Distillery the year prior. There was one man in charge of the operation at the time, and that same man remains in charge today—Jimmy

Russell. You can tell me this, that, or the other reason Austin, Nichols might've acquired the J.T.S. Brown & Sons Distillery. Whatever fact or figure you throw at me, it all boils down to Jimmy.

Stay with me. You'll see.

Surely, you've purchased a supermarket's store-brand product at some point in time. For example, instead of Lucky Charms cereal, you might've purchased "Marshmallow Mates" or "Magic Stars." Essentially, that's how Wild Turkey started, as a store-brand whiskey.

From the late 1800s to the early 1900s, Austin, Nichols & Co. was the largest grocery wholesaler in the world. They were the Costco of its day (sans retail-consumer relationship). By 1934, the tide had turned, however. Grocery distribution wasn't the same business it had been. "Five & Dimes" had taken over, merchandise was no longer kept behind a clerk's counter, and the overall retailer-wholesaler relationship evolved. Austin, Nichols felt

that shift and entered wine and spirits distribution as a means of diversifi-
cation. By 1939, wine and spirits would be their sole focus.

While distributing spirits of various labels was certainly lucrative
post-Prohibition, Austin, Nichols & Co. needed a house-brand whiskey to
garner profits and meet the rising demand for Kentucky straight bourbon.
The story goes that in the late 1930s, on a company hunting trip in South
Carolina, Wild Turkey Bourbon was conceived. We've heard the tale many
times, but in my mind, it's nothing compared to the story I'm telling you now.

Remember, stay with me.

Austin, Nichols' Wild Turkey 101 first hit shelves in 1942. It was a
respectable success and continued as such for decades. So much so that
it only made sense for Austin, Nichols to move from sourced whiskey to
a distillery of their own. By the 1950s, the Anderson County Distillery in
Tyrone, Kentucky, was producing some of the best bourbon around, rivaling
whiskey from established names like Stitzel-Weller and National Distillers.
Austin, Nichols often purchased bourbon from Anderson County (later
operating as J.T.S. Brown & Sons) for Wild Turkey 101. As a result, it soon
became the choice profile for their brand. What made this desirable profile
so special? Jimmy Russell.

In 1954, James "Jimmy" C. Russell began his career at Anderson County
Distilling Co., which four years earlier had been operating as Ripy Brothers
Distillery. Jimmy learned the art of bourbon production from Master
Distiller Bill Hughes, who I've been told was quite the character, and Ernest
W. Ripy, Jr., grandson of famed Lawrenceburg distiller T.B. Ripy. Back in
those days, everything was done the old-fashioned way—no shortcuts,
no compromises.

By 1967, through years of hard work and dedication, the title of Master
Distiller was granted to Jimmy Russell. The newly appointed master dis-
tiller not only kept production standards high, he effectively raised the bar.
Austin, Nichols took note, and in 1971 the distillery became the Austin,

Nichols Distilling Co. Wild Turkey 101 now had a permanent home and a once-in-a-lifetime steward in Jimmy Russell. The rest, as they say, is history.

What do you think of when you sip Wild Turkey 101? Do you think of a grocery wholesaler? Do you consider yourself sipping a distributor's house label? No. You think Wild Turkey. You think Russell. And that's because Jimmy Russell, through strong leadership and uncompromising craftsmanship, made Wild Turkey the household name it is today. Sure, Austin, Nichols & Co., Pernod Ricard, and Campari all made considerable financial investments over the years, but Jimmy changed the brand forever. Without Jimmy Russell, I'd argue that Wild Turkey would likely be a dead label. Hell, I'm almost certain it would be. It's a quirky name that's struggled against misconceptions for years. Yet, it's delicious and unfailingly reliable. We buy Wild Turkey because it tastes good—because it's of high quality—and we have Jimmy Russell to thank for that.

Speaking of quality, I'd say it's about time for a whiskey review. Thanks to a generous bourbon friend (appreciate it, T.J.), I have the opportunity to taste a Wild Turkey 101 from 1972 (at least thereabouts). There's no precise science to dating bottles. Even in its pristine shape, this bottle still has several indicators to consider. First off, the glass stamp carries a weak strike on the bottle's underside. It appears to read "69," but this can't be a 1969 release because the label clearly reads "Lawrenceburg, KY." Prior to 1972 (and somewhat in transition through early 1972), Wild Turkey labels stated "New York, NY" (and "Brooklyn, NY" prior to that). Also supporting an early 1970's bottling is an IRS tax strip (instead of a post-1976 ATF strip) and a "sans-Turkey" reverse label. All things considered, for the purposes of this review, I'm going with "about 1972."

Wild Turkey 101 (about 1972)

SPIRIT: Kentucky straight bourbon whiskey

PROOF: 101

AGE: eight years

MISC.: bottled by the Austin, Nichols Distilling Co., Lawrenceburg, KY

tasted neat in a Glencairn Glass after a few minutes rest…

COLOR: rose copper

NOSE: (dusty with sweet minerality) butterscotch, fruitcake, cherry-vanilla, candied almonds, caramel drizzle, musty oak, tilled soil, tobacco, maple, hints of pineapple and chewable vitamins

TASTE: (vibrant and tart) sweet minerals, tangy vanilla, fruity and funky oak, orange peel, caramel candy, herbal tea, lemon icing, peppery spice

FINISH: medium-long, sweet and spicy—fruit candy, butterscotch, orange/lemon zest; herbal and floral spice, nutmeg, musty oak, Red Hots cinnamon candy, faint leather

OVERALL:

Well, this is a surprise. Sweet minerals… a substantial volume of sweet minerals. I've experienced similar profiles before. A 1979 Wild Turkey 101 8-Year immediately comes to mind, as does a 1989 101/8 (though it had only traces of minerality). Outside of that, there's plenty of fruity vanilla, butterscotch candy, and herbal/floral spice to keep one going back for more. Even so, it's hard to escape the rather dominant tangy mineral notes. A wonderfully complex and quirky pour; a rare treat I'm grateful to experience.

SWEET MINERALS & BUTTERSCOTCH

What's going on? Why doesn't this sip like typical dusty Wild Turkey? For starters, we must consider the possibility of sourced whiskey. After all, the label says, "bottled by," and 1972 is a few years away from Eddie's time at the distillery. Eddie Russell has stated publicly that whiskey hasn't been sourced for Wild Turkey products since the day he started in 1981. Jimmy's not talking. But don't take that for evasiveness. That's just Jimmy being Jimmy.

Do I believe this 1972 Wild Turkey 101 contains sourced bourbon? At one time I might've said yes. Now, I'm not so sure.

The Wild Turkey sourced whiskey argument starts losing water by the time we reach the 1970s. From all references I can find, Austin, Nichols & Co. was more than pleased with the whiskey distilled at Anderson County/J.T.S. Brown in the 1960s. Besides, Jimmy is very particular about his bourbon. From what I've gathered, he strongly prefers using his own whiskey to fill Wild Turkey bottles—and did so even back then. We know that sourced whiskey was acquired from Old Boone by Austin, Nichols, though much of it was left unused. In fact, many of those unused barrels became the first Pappy Van Winkle, as reported by bourbon historian Michael Veach.

> It took a few years but [Julian Van Winkle] finally found the bourbon for this new brand. He had managed to purchase the last of the Old Boone whiskey from its owners, Wild Turkey [Austin, Nichols & Co.]. They had purchased the bourbon in the early '70s, when the brand was growing, and they needed whiskey to fill bottles in new markets. They purchased their own distillery at that time and the Old Boone whiskey was not needed [. . .] so they sold it to Julian.

According to Veach, Austin, Nichols & Co. originally purchased barrels from Old Boone to "fill bottles in new markets." What that means exactly, I'm uncertain. But he goes on to say that after purchasing J.T.S. Brown & Sons, the Old Boone barrels were no longer necessary. Does that mean early-1970s Wild Turkey 101 is sourced or isn't? I'm wagering not.

That leaves no explanation for the atypical profile I'm experiencing with this 1972 expression, right? Maybe, maybe not. If there's one thing I've learned firsthand from Jimmy Russell, it's how Wild Turkey pulls its barrels.

Last November, I was talking with the Russells about choice or favorite rickhouses and why barrels weren't pulled from them every year. That's when Jimmy chimed in. He explained that, each year, certain rickhouses are harvested for barrels. In other words, Wild Turkey barrels are pulled from select rickhouses each year according to age and taste.

Think of years as maturation seasons. For example, this season (2017–2018) Tyrone rickhouses B, D, H, and K can be found as single-barrel selections, as well as Camp Nelson A and F. Last season (2016-2017), Tyrone G, K, M, and O barrels were available as single-barrel selections. Using that logic, it's very possible that whichever rickhouses were harvested in 1972 (and/or 1979, 1989, etc.) simply contained barrels showcasing a fruity-mineral profile. Since today's barrels vary by rickhouse, it only makes sense that yesterday's barrels experienced the same.

Reflecting back on all of this, I can't help but imagine how exciting the early 1970s must've been for Jimmy Russell. He would've been a few years

COULD YOU DO WHAT JIMMY'S DONE? COULD ANYONE?

younger than me at the time, and that resonates. According to Eddie Russell, Jimmy ran it all as Master Distiller, Plant Manager, Human Resources Director, etc. If the distillery failed, Wild Turkey would fail, leaving only one man to blame. Thankfully, that never happened. Even through the infamous Glut Era, when numerous distilleries closed their doors forever, Jimmy persevered. And more impressively, he took a distributor's whiskey label and turned it into the everyman's quality pour.

So, the next time you're at Costco and you pass a Kirkland's whiskey bottle (Costco's house brand), consider how difficult it would be to bring that label to the mainstream, to make it recognizable, popular, and a well-respected bourbon worldwide. Could you do what Jimmy's done? Could anyone? It's hard to say. Yet, as I finish my last sip of this 1972 Wild Turkey 101, I find comfort in the fact that this label will be around for decades to come. Be it through Eddie, Bruce, JoAnn, or names of generations unseen, Wild Turkey is rooted in Jimmy. Wild Turkey is Russell.

WILD TURKEY AMERICAN SPIRIT

Wild Turkey American Spirit

In September 2018, Jimmy and Eddie Russell celebrated their combined 101st year of service in the bourbon industry—all at Wild Turkey, to boot! To my knowledge, there hasn't been a father-son distilling team with this same tenure. A few months beforehand, I challenged my Patreon community, also known as "Russell's Renegades," to come up with a special gift to mark the occasion for Jimmy and Eddie. Together, we did.

We scoured our individual collections to amass a library of epic Wild Turkey bourbon samples. The list was a "who's who" of legendary expressions: vintage eight-year 101s, "Cheesy Gold Foil," "Donut," etc. Housed in two extraordinary, handcrafted boxes by my good friend James Richards, it was an impressive assembly to say the least. If only I'd been there to see Jimmy and Eddie receive them! Regardless, they were accepted with great thanks and humility. Jimmy's reaction served as the inspiration for this post. dj

NOVEMBER 13, 2018

When it comes to Wild Turkey limited editions, I don't think there's one I'm asked about more than American Spirit. Many times I've been queried, and many times I've replied, "Very sorry, I haven't tried that one yet."

I haven't been avoiding American Spirit; I just have so many wonderful Turkeys to enjoy that I rarely seek out a single dusty expression (and when I do, "Donut" and "Cheesy Gold Foil" are typically front of the line). More often than not, I'm perfectly content purchasing Russell's Reserve Single Barrel private selections. But sometimes fortune comes your way, as it did with this American Spirit. I may not have the fancy box, but I definitely have the best part!

What makes American Spirit special enough to warrant so many inquiries? For starters, it's the only bottled-in-bond Wild Turkey expression to date. It's not the only bottled-in-bond whiskey ever produced at the distillery, however. I've seen bottles from the old Anderson County Distillery days with DSP-KY-67 on the labels. They're not the easiest bottles to find, but they're out there. American Spirit is also the first 100-proof bourbon released under the Wild Turkey or Russell's Reserve brand (as opposed to the signature 101 proof). Of course, one could argue this simply goes hand in hand with being a bottled-in-bond expression.

You may be wondering what "bottled in bond" means. While there's very little a quick Google search can't solve, I'll gladly spare you the time and point you in the right direction. Here's a quick definition courtesy of bourbon historian Michael Veach. Regarding said expressions, the U.S. Bottled-In-Bond Act of 1897 states:

All of the whiskey in the bottle comes from the same distillery, made in the same season, aged for at least four years in a government bonded warehouse, and bottled at 100 proof with nothing other than water added to the whiskey.

So, without legal exception, American Spirit was distilled at Wild Turkey in a single season. It's stated as fifteen years aged and bottled at 100 proof, so the label specs check out. According to Eddie Russell, every warehouse owned and operated by Wild Turkey (on and off site) is government bonded. Taking all locations into consideration, the chance of narrowing down a particular maturation site for American Spirit (outside of Jimmy and Eddie's recollection) is fairly slim.

I have a lot more to say about Wild Turkey American Spirit, but before doing so, I think it's best to provide some tasting notes for reference. Let's pour!

Wild Turkey American Spirit – 2007 Master Distiller Selection

SPIRIT: Kentucky straight bourbon whiskey

PROOF: 100

AGE: fifteen years

MISC.: bottled in bond; distilled by the Austin, Nichols Distilling Co., Lawrenceburg, KY, DSP-KY-67

tasted neat in a Glencairn Glass after a few minutes rest...

COLOR: rich copper

NOSE: (classic Wild Turkey) honey-maple, fruity vanilla, fragrant oak, caramel drizzle, orange peel, herbal/floral spice, nutmeg, hints of cinnamon

TASTE: vanilla extract, honey-maple, caramel candy, sweet musty oak, nutmeg, peppery spice, faint citrus and leather

FINISH: long, laced with spice—vanilla, nutmeg, caramel, butter toffee, oak char, leather, clove, cinnamon

OVERALL: Signature Jimmy Russell. In fact, I don't think I've ever had a Wild Turkey expression so true to Jimmy's reported profile preference. Diamond Anniversary comes close, but it's no American Spirit. While both are rooted in the classic Wild Turkey profile, Diamond is of a lighter variety. American Spirit, on the other hand, has similar notes but with increased depth, ABV, and overall maturity. It's a damn fine pour—not necessarily my personal favorite Wild Turkey expression but a damn fine bourbon nonetheless.

As I sit here sipping American Spirit, reflecting on my notes, and gauging my impression, I can't help but think of Jimmy. Just a week ago, generous patrons and friends delivered a special gift to Jimmy Russell for his and Eddie Russell's 101 years of combined industry service. After gathering up samples of top-quality Wild Turkey expressions, spanning the 1970s through the early 2010s, they were labeled and placed in a custom-designed box meticulously crafted by the talented James Richards. A masterful work for the world's longest-tenured master distiller.

And Jimmy? Well, he couldn't have been more thrilled about his gift. He sat in his living room that Sunday afternoon, admiring the box and going through each sample one by one. Jimmy had a lot to say about many of them, but none as much as American Spirit. In fact, he made it crystal clear: American Spirit is his favorite Wild Turkey expression. That's something to remember and take note of. Regardless of what you, I, or anyone else thinks of American Spirit, in Jimmy's heart, it's his best.

What makes American Spirit special? The answer is much simpler than late-nineteenth-century laws or double-digit age statements. It's Jimmy Russell's favorite bourbon. I think that says it all.

REGARDLESS OF WHAT YOU, I, OR ANYONE ELSE THINKS OF AMERICAN SPIRIT, IN JIMMY'S HEART, IT'S HIS BEST

PHOTO BY CHAD PERKINS

The Best of 2018

If ever there were a big year for Wild Turkey, it was 2018. I had my first Russell's Reserve private selection experience; the distillery released two unconventional expressions, Longbranch and Master's Keep Revival; and the course of the year revealed an overall uptick in quality for core expressions. My blog was growing, and I'd finally settled into a weekly publishing flow. Last, but not least, work had begun on my first Wild Turkey book manuscript. Everything was looking up. It seemed only prudent to take an appreciative look back. dj

DECEMBER 18, 2018

Another year has come and gone, and with it some truly remarkable whiskeys. Going into 2018, I had high hopes for Wild Turkey. Not only were those hopes exceeded, in many ways they arrived with a personal touch. (Happy 101st anniversary, Jimmy and Eddie!)

To say that this year was rewarding as a Wild Turkey enthusiast would be an understatement. This year was phenomenal. Now it's time to showcase a handful of noteworthy whiskeys that made it so. Here's The Best of Wild Turkey 2018.

Best Design (2018)
Wild Turkey
Longbranch

Spring of 2018 saw the arrival of the "Lincoln Town Car of Bourbon": Wild Turkey Longbranch. It seems the company's famous creative director finally found an alright (alright, alright) bottle of his own—a unique combination of eight-year bourbon and Texas mesquite refinement. While as a diehard enthusiast's neat sipper, I didn't find Longbranch all that appealing, I did find it outperformed notable whiskeys in its class, specifically Jack Daniel's Gentleman Jack and Jim Beam's Basil Hayden's. Longbranch's design, however, established a new standard for celebrity whiskey expressions.

Truth be told, Longbranch's glass bottle was originally intended as a Wild Turkey Kentucky Spirit redesign (a 2016 TTB filing helps to illustrate). But when you have an A-list creative director, you need an A-grade bottle for his whiskey. The intended Kentucky Spirit redesign took a back seat to Longbranch, and it only made sense. It's hefty, like Texas, yet simplistic and graceful in its display of Kentucky's finest within. With antique-style embossing, classy minimalist labeling, and a solid wood stopper with the girth and feel of a small oak branch, Longbranch looks undeniably handsome on any whiskey shelf.

BEST CORE EXPRESSION (2018)
WILD TURKEY 101

Old Faithful, The Daily, the Kickin' Chicken . . . yes, I'm talking about the stalwart everyman's pour, Wild Turkey 101. You might be asking, *why 101 for Best Core Expression of 2018?* After all, I've yet to formally review a 2018 bottle. True, but that doesn't mean I haven't been sipping them! At this point, I've tasted enough bottles to know that when it comes to Wild Turkey 101, all batches aren't created equal. Without doubt, modern 101 is consistently good, but find yourself the right bottle and you'll be rewarded with a strikingly flavorful and balanced pour (all for less than $25).

While Wild Turkey 101 has remained a staple in my home for years now, these mid to late 2018 bottles are something to be treasured. But you don't have to take my word for it. No sir, no ma'am. Next time you're at your local bottle shop, pick up a bottle. Grab a 375ml or mini if you want a minimal investment. The key is locating a bottle code beginning with LL/G. "G" denotes 2018, and the letter following is the month ("A" is January, "B" is February, etc.). Buy several different dates and taste them side by side. You might be surprised.

Best Straight Bourbon (2018)
Russell's Reserve Single Barrel Bourbon
(Master Distiller Selection)

Twenty-eighteen was arguably the year for Russell's Reserve Single Barrel private selections. It all started with Lexington Bourbon Society's "Final Pour." But while that release set a high bar in quality, it did little to prepare me for the choice barrels that followed: Motor Supply Co.'s rickhouse D barrel, Beast Masters' "That Old Kentucky Chew" (rickhouse B), Barrels & Brews' "Haters Gonna Hate" (rickhouse H), and last but certainly not least, the distillery exclusive Master Distiller Selection (rickhouse D).

What made the 2018 Master Distiller Selection so special? Well, it's not often that you find a single barrel selected by four esteemed Kentucky master distillers: Jimmy and Eddie Russell, Fred Noe of Jim Beam, and Chris Morris of Woodford Reserve. Talk about a lineup! It was such a unique event that I had no choice but to take a few "creative liberties" with its backstory. As for the bourbon itself . . . rich and robust Tyrone-aged excellence. A near-perfect combination of ideal maturity, intense complexity, and rare balance. Well done, gentlemen.

BEST STRAIGHT RYE (2018)
WILD TURKEY 101 RYE

Twenty-seventeen's Best Straight Rye holds on to its crown! Having discussed this expression several times this year, I don't think there's much more to say about Wild Turkey 101 Rye, though there's one thing worth repeating: it's hands down the best Kentucky straight rye whiskey in its price tier. If you can find something better for the money, I'd certainly like to hear about it. (Don't worry. My inbox isn't sweating it.)

BEST SINGLE BARREL (2018)
SINGLE CASK NATION WILD TURKEY
(BARREL #16-313)

Those J&J Spirits boys have done it again! There was a time I thought that Single Cask Nation and Whisky Jewbilee bottlings had a slight advantage over Wild Turkey branded selections simply because J&J bottles at barrel proof. While I can't dismiss that argument altogether, I can say that, personally, I've come to realize that significant mojo comes from Joshua Hatton and Jason Johnstone-Yellin.

Two Single Cask Nation bottles stood well above the single barrel crowd this year (a tough year to stand out in, I might add). Barrel #1075 is a funky and fruity rickhouse K flavor bomb. Originally marked as "rejected" by the distillery, Joshua and Jason couldn't resist tasting a misfit barrel (and I'm so glad they took that chance). The result is in many ways a throwback to the old-school "Wild Turkey Funk." An amazingly unique and contemplative whiskey. But just when you thought J&J Spirits had their shining "chance-of-a-lifetime" barrel moment, they had a hell of a surprise waiting for us . . . barrel #16-313.

Single Cask Nation barrel #16-313 is a bourbon tour de force. The label states "a bourbon for Scotch drinkers," but don't let that statement fool you. This Wild Turkey barrel tastes nothing like distilled malted barley; that said, it has every bit of the layered complexity and timeless charm of a highly cherished bottle of vintage Scotch whisky. It has dark chocolate. It has pipe tobacco. It has molasses, horehound candy, sweet smoke, and countless thought-provoking notes that ultimately leave an indelible impression bordering whiskey perfection. It's the Best Single Barrel of 2018 and J&J Spirits (and Wild Turkey) should be proud.

BEST WHISKEY OVERALL (2018)
WILD TURKEY MASTER'S KEEP REVIVAL

We all knew it was coming, but no one (not even a Turkey fanatic like me) was prepared for how incredibly delicious Wild Turkey Master's Keep Revival would be. Talk about a complex whiskey! The thing I love most about Revival is that it's so "outside of the box," yet at the same time it ironically isn't. Scratching your head? Think of it like this: while twenty-year-old Spanish Oloroso Sherry casks undoubtedly added their "Old World" signature touch to the twelve- to fifteen-year bourbon, Revival stayed well within the beloved classic Wild Turkey profile. We have Master Distiller Eddie Russell and his hardworking team to thank for that.

From day one, Revival was Eddie's baby—and boy, did he raise it well. There's plenty of brands finishing whiskeys, primarily rye, in ex-wine casks. From craft distilleries to major producers, some do it better than others, yet few do it well with bourbon. What Eddie accomplished with Revival is a masterwork. An impeccable example of dedication and craftsmanship that will be revered for many years to come. It's my favorite whiskey of 2018, and it deserves every bit of praise a whiskey enthusiast can give. Congratulations, Eddie.

A most sincere thanks to everyone that helped make 2018 a fantastic year for Wild Turkey. From the Russell family and the entire distillery crew in Tyrone, to the kind folks at Campari America, I thank you. From Joshua and Jason of J&J Spirits to Fred Noe and Chris Morris, y'all picked some stellar barrels, and I thank you. And finally, to all of my bourbon family, friends, patrons, supporters, followers, and readers, I wholeheartedly thank you; 2018 has been wonderful, and I can't say thank you enough. Here's to 2019 . . . cheers!

WILD TURKEY BLENDS

Wild Turkey Blends

As strange as it sounds, few blog entries garner readership like those concerning whiskey blends. I'm not exactly sure why. I assume readers find the same enjoyment I do, or maybe they like making new whiskeys from whiskeys they already have at home. Whatever the reason, blending is as fun to experiment with as it is to write about. This was my second attempt at sharing custom Wild Turkey blends. It certainly won't be my last. dj

JANUARY 22, 2019

B ack in September 2018, I published "Hacking Wild Turkey." It was a fun little piece all about experimentation and blending. Today's post is a similar adventure.

I'm always on the search for new Wild Turkey flavor profiles. Purchasing single-barrel expressions is one way to get there (arguably the best way in terms of quality). But buying single-barrel expressions can get rather expensive. And once you pop the top, what you have is all you'll get (for better or worse). Blending, on the other hand, offers flexibility on a much wider scale—from budget to premium. Often, you'll fail before you succeed. But, when you finally do craft a winner . . . well, it's truly special.

Today, I'll be sharing blending ideas not covered in last year's post. Whether you appreciate these or not, I hope they inspire you to try your own Wild Turkey blends. Remember that there are no rules and you're never "wasting" whiskey. Whiskey is made to be consumed and enjoyed. If you're enjoying the blending process, you're not wasting a drop. Also, there's no reward without sacrifice; if you never take the chance, you never experience the outcome (miserable or marvelous). But before you start emptying your favorite bottles to fashion the ultimate Wild Turkey whiskey, consider trying one of these blends first. I think you might just come away happy.

LONGBREED

Looking for a way to spice up that bottle of Longbranch? Unless you're a fan of mellow pours, I'd imagine you are. Here's a simple blend I recently discovered that may just have you reaching for that Longbranch bottle more frequently.

* 50% Wild Turkey Longbranch
* 50% Wild Turkey Rare Breed 116.8

Net proof = 101.4

The first thing interesting about this blend is its net proof: almost 101 exactly. With Longbranch being a reported eight-year bourbon, and Rare Breed a reported batch of six-, eight-, and twelve-year bourbon, you're bringing the overall maturation closer to a well-aged medium.

Second, each bourbon shines in different phases. I find that Rare Breed dominates the blend's nose, while Longbranch makes its presence known on the palate (primarily in mouthfeel). The finish is a graceful unity of the two with elements of each sharing the spotlight. It's certainly more mellow than Rare Breed alone, yet notably longer and spicier than Longbranch. Overall, a flavorful, easy-sipping straight bourbon blend, and one I highly recommend for anyone with a bottle of each whiskey on hand.

Rye-Deemed

As many of you know, I'm not the biggest fan of Wild Turkey Forgiven. It's not bad; it's just a bit young and under-proofed for my preference. That said, you like what you like, and if you happen to like Forgiven, there's no problem with that at all. I even posted a little hack for you last year if you're running low and don't want to search secondary markets for another bottle (not that it would cost you an insane premium, but anyways).

Traditionally, I've had very little luck when blending Wild Turkey straight bourbon and rye whiskeys. I've tried 50/50 Wild Turkey 101 bourbon and rye, 50/50 Russell's Reserve Single Barrel bourbon and rye, and several other 50/50 combos with various expressions and ratios. Many times I've failed to reach a "this is a remarkable" blend. It seemed Wild Turkey straight whiskeys were best mixed with their relative types—bourbon with bourbon, rye with rye.

Thankfully, a Turkey friend from across the pond offered me a mystery sample that completely changed my way of thinking (thanks, Lee). After a long night of writing, I poured the curious sample and found I liked it quite a bit. I knew it was Wild Turkey, but which Turkey was it? The answer shocked me. It was a blend I'd tried numerous times before with little success . . .

50/50 Wild Turkey 101 bourbon and rye. Maybe not knowing what I was tasting made a difference? Maybe it was timing? Maybe it was attitude? I can only guess. But all said and done, it accomplished one important thing: it showed that Wild Turkey bourbon and rye blends can work.

Fast forward to this past week . . . I tried a new Wild Turkey bourbon and rye blend that's magnificent. You may or may not agree (and that's fine), but regardless of what others think, this is a blend I'll keep around here forward. I call it "Rye-deemed," and I think you'll love it.

* 50% Wild Turkey 101 Rye
* 25% Wild Turkey Rare Breed 116.8
* 25% Wild Turkey Master's Keep 17-Year*

Net proof = 101.4

If you don't have the seventeen-year Master's Keep, try Master's Keep Decades. You'll get a bit less oak, but a little more ABV (105.7 proof).

Hello, layers of spicy sweetness! Say what you will about this blend, but you'll have to agree with me on one thing: it's harmonious. While the previously discussed "Longbreed" has tasting phases where each component expression stands out over the other, Rye-deemed smells, feels, and tastes as a well-executed blend should, with the sum of all parts working together to create something extraordinary. But don't take my word for it. Roll the dice and give it a try!

INFINITE GOBBLE

Infinity bottles. We've all tried them; we've all been mildly impressed. When I first started experimenting with infinity bottles years ago, there was no real thought process. I'd take the last sip or two of a bottle or sample and add it to my infinity blend. Simple. It didn't matter what type of whiskey. Proof and maturity weren't factors of interest either. If a whiskey reached its end, into the infinity bottle it went. And what was the result? A batch of confusion that never really "added up." Sure, there were moments of hope, but never a feeling of confidence or accomplishment. What was I doing wrong? Is this how all infinity whiskeys taste?

That's when I realized you have to set boundaries. For me, that came together with my love for Wild Turkey. And while they haven't all been successes, in time I slowly figured out how to keep a damn good Turkey-based infinity bottle.

Here's what works for me:

1. Stick with one type of straight whiskey (bourbon with bourbon, or rye with rye).

2. Avoid finished whiskeys (such as Master's Keep Revival). Once you add a finished whiskey, you can't "roll back" the profile.

3. Avoid low-proof whiskeys, such as Wild Turkey 81 or 81 Rye. One exception is Master's Keep 17-Year, which I'll discuss shortly.

4. If possible, try to keep the overall maturity balanced. This is more applicable to bourbon blends than rye blends. While the majority of what you'll add will fall between six to eight years, try to increase the maturity every so often with ten-plus-year expressions.

5. Keep the proof above 100. I mean, this is Wild Turkey after all. But seriously, keeping an infinity bottle over 100 proof promotes greater texture and complexity. Besides, you can always dilute with water in your glass post pour.

While I encourage you to create your own set of infinity bottle guidelines, following (or at least hovering around) the ones I've listed above should yield satisfactory results. The main thing is to take your time and have fun. Taste as you go. Stay critical, yet keep an open mind and don't give up. I'm positive you'll eventually turn out something noteworthy. And when you do, always remember to share with friends!

Working with Expressions

The final topic I'll touch on today is which expressions I most often employ in my blending experiments, as well as how and why I use them. While this list is far from all-inclusive, it showcases the bottles I incorporate most often. Thankfully, the majority are standard expressions that can easily be found at suggested retail price.

WILD TURKEY 101 (OR 101 RYE). This is a good place to start for any whiskey blend, as it offers quality core notes with moderate maturity.

WILD TURKEY RARE BREED 116.8. If you ever feel your blend is falling flat or lacking vibrancy or "kick," a little Rare Breed goes a very long way.

RUSSELL'S RESERVE 10-YEAR. If you ever need to bring the heat of your blend down but don't want to sacrifice maturity, consider adding the 90-proof Russell's Reserve 10-Year.

WILD TURKEY MASTER'S KEEP 17-YEAR. This is my secret weapon when it comes to blending. Master's Keep's fragrant oak and layered spice can really take a so-so blend and make it extra special. And while it's only 86.8 proof, it's near-batch-proof (I believe the actual batch proof was 88.4). My point is, you're not adding water. You're adding a full-flavored mature bourbon whiskey instead. How is that ever a bad thing? Oh, and if you can't find the seventeen-year Master's Keep, Decades is an appropriate substitution.

RUSSELL'S RESERVE SINGLE BARREL (bourbon or rye private selections). The beauty of Russell's Reserve Single Barrel, especially private selections, is their wonderful profile variance. Each private selection in your collection has something unique to offer. Refer to your tasting notes and choose wisely.

Thanks for reading. I hope you found this post informative, or at least started you thinking about the possibilities that await you in your cabinet. So, what are you waiting for? Grab an empty bottle or decanter and blend away! Maybe begin with sample bottles before committing to larger batches. It's all up to you. There are no rules. But no matter what you do, stay focused and keep it fun. Cheers!

MY BLENDS

This bourbon whiskey was bottled
from barrel no.
a warehouse   on rick no.
ed for the bourbon connois
alc./vol. (101) pro

WILD
TURKEY®

SINGLE BARREL BOURBON

ECTED BY OUR MASTER DISTIL

KENTUCKY
SPIRIT

Single Barrel

KENTUCKY STRAIGHT BOURBON WHISKEY

750ml

R.I.P. Wild Turkey Kentucky Spirit

I can't think of a single Wild Turkey expression that's delivered more of an emotional rollercoaster than Kentucky Spirit. When the classic "fantail" bottle design was discontinued in early 2019, it appeared the final straw for an already floundering product. Reading back over this post, I can feel the immense disappointment I harbored at the time.

It's been nearly three years since I wrote this piece, and while I'm not thrilled with the new "repurposed Rare Breed" bottle, I've moved on. My focus now lies where it should've then—the whiskey itself. That doesn't mean I've made peace with the redesign ... I've just accepted that it's second in importance to the quality of the bourbon.

Writing this note in 2022, I'm happy to report that Kentucky Spirit is doing well, arguably better than it has done in years. I don't believe its success has any-thing to do with aesthetics; rather, it's the impres-siveness of the barrels selected for bottling making the difference. Let's hope this trend continues for many years to come. But, for the record, I still wouldn't mind seeing that classic fantail bottle again. dj

First, I should apologize for the grim headline. Wild Turkey Kentucky Spirit isn't going anywhere—not yet at least. But I have to admit, I worry for its future.

Before I dig in, it's imperative for me to state I mean no offense to the Russells, Wild Turkey, or Campari. I have the highest respect for what you do (all of you) and appreciate your hard work and dedication on a daily basis. That's not lip service, that's fact.

The Campari years have been great for Wild Turkey. That cannot be denied. The brand is in so many ways shining brighter than ever before, but if you reflect on bourbon's colorful past, you'll notice that times of great success are often when things are most overlooked. How does this relate to Wild Turkey, specifically Wild Turkey Kentucky Spirit? Let's take a look.

How It Was

Wild Turkey Kentucky Spirit was created in 1994. Some cite 1995 for its official release, but the first bottles were filled and labeled in 1994. In almost every way, Kentucky Spirit was a direct response to Elmer T. Lee's crowning achievement, Blanton's. With its decorative box, ornate bottle, handwritten specs, and hefty pewter top, the original Wild Turkey Kentucky Spirit was remarkably similar. And the whiskey inside? Marvelous.

With the exception of Wild Turkey Kentucky Legend and the duty-free exclusive Wild Turkey Heritage, Kentucky Spirit would remain Wild Turkey's sole single-barrel expression for roughly nineteen years.

Everything changed with the introduction of Russell's Reserve Single Barrel Bourbon in 2013. Wild Turkey fans now had a single-barrel expression that was non-chill filtered and even closer to barrel strength at 110 proof. I'm not certain it was an immediate success, but I can say that by the time the private barrel program started the following year, it didn't take long for the expression to garner attention and critical praise. In fact, I think the turning point came around the end of 2016, when author Fred Minnick favorably reviewed a Lincoln Road Package Store Russell's Reserve selection via Twitter and, later, *Whisky Advocate Magazine*. Not only did that review help put Jamie Farris on the national bourbon map, it did the same for Russell's Reserve Single Barrel. From that point forward, Russell's Reserve Single Barrel (particularly private selections) were on fire.

But what about Kentucky Spirit? It was also available as a private selection by 2014. Why didn't you hear more about it? Why were so many retail Kentucky Spirit bottles sitting on shelves? The answer is twofold: profile and popularity.

If you've ever had the opportunity to taste Wild Turkey Kentucky Spirit releases from years past, you've surely noticed the profile changed. Yes, it's a single-barrel expression, but that's not what I'm referring to. What I'm saying is that, in a general sense, the profile drifted over time. Like every long-tenured Wild Turkey expression (and really, any other distillery's long-tenured expression), gone were the classic and "dusty-esque" notes of the past. Kentucky Spirit became more refined—"lighter," for lack of a better word. While that might appeal to some folks, most whiskey enthusiasts found themselves gravitating toward Russell's Reserve Single Barrel, with its robust and fuller-flavored profile. Kentucky

Spirit, on the other hand, essentially became a single-barrel version of Wild Turkey 101—at double the price (or more).

So, it begs the question: What's Wild Turkey Kentucky Spirit's target consumer audience? Casual drinkers? At its price point and specs, I highly doubt it. Casual neat or rocks sippers? Maybe, but then Russell's Reserve 10-Year and Wild Turkey Longbranch easily fill that role. They're also cheaper and more widely available expressions. So, that leaves whiskey enthusiasts.

Do you think Kentucky Spirit is an ideal whiskey enthusiast's pour in today's highly competitive market? Probably not. While I don't have inside information or sales reports to back it up, I'm willing to bet the numbers line up with that assertion.

How It Is

Here we are in 2019, and things aren't looking very promising. Gone is the iconic tail-feather glass that's defined Kentucky Spirit from its beginning. In its place, we basically have a modern Rare Breed bottle with new stickers. To me, it seems as if the designers might have been going for a Russell's Reserve 1998/2002 vibe, but in reality, it appears more like a homemade infinity bottle. Truth be told, this wasn't Kentucky Spirit's original redesign. That went to Longbranch, as discussed in past blog entries.

I promise you this: today will be my last official rant regarding Kentucky Spirit's (arguably lazy) bottle redesign. Honestly, I feel a little guilty. It seems there's actually a few folks excited about it. They're called Camparistas (Campari reps). I've commented on their Instagram posts (as well as replies to mine), openly sharing my thoughts on the redesign on more than one occasion. I almost never feel good about it afterwards. Camparistas have such positive enthusiasm for their company and its brands. It's as if I'm telling kids the hard truth about Santa Claus. And no matter what I say or how I say it, I just don't think social media commentary will change Kentucky Spirit's fate.

But Wild Turkey Kentucky Spirit isn't dead; it's merely surviving on life support. Don't blame that solely on the bottle redesign. It's far too early in the game to see if that hurts or helps sales. I just don't think the new look is doing the expression any favors.

Outside of presentation, Kentucky Spirit still has to compete with Russell's Reserve Single Barrel and Wild Turkey 101, not to mention countless other (considerably cheaper) bourbon expressions at or above 100 proof. Again, things aren't looking very promising.

So, what can be done? What should be done? Let's explore some options and potential solutions. Perhaps the fate of Wild Turkey Kentucky Spirit can be altered.

How It Could Be

As it stands today, there's only three things I can think of (outside of price) that could potentially save Kentucky Spirit, and the first is painfully obvious: design a nicer bottle.

I understand there are reasons why the classic tail-feather bottle is no longer an option, but that doesn't mean something of comparable beauty can't be found. How about a throwback bottle design, like export Kentucky Legend (101 proof) or export Tradition? Or maybe something entirely new? Hell, the sky's the limit. Campari is perfectly capable of expert design. Why make Kentucky Spirit the lazy exception to such high standards?

Second, there's no reason to keep Wild Turkey Kentucky Spirit a chill-filtered bourbon whiskey. Making Kentucky Spirit a non-chill-filtered expression would give it a nice advantage over the notably cheaper alternative of Wild Turkey 101. In fact, I'd argue the change would make

Kentucky Spirit more appealing to both vendors and consumers considering private barrel selections.

Third, make Kentucky Spirit's barrel specs more attractive to whiskey enthusiasts. This could be done by simply adding a "barreled on" date. The bottling date has been there since 1994, why not (finally) tell consumers when it was barreled? After all, if we're in agreement that Kentucky Spirit is aiming for whiskey enthusiasts, why not shoot for the bullseye? You could even "split the arrow" and add the original barrel proof. Bourbon nerds love details—Turkey nerds probably more so. A few numbers added to a paper label might just equal a few numbers added to the company ledger.

How It Should Be

At this point, I've covered what could be done. Now for what should be done. I'll warn you: die-hard Turkey fans may find my solution sobering.

Pull the plug.

You read that right. Maybe Wild Turkey Kentucky Spirit, at least as we know it today, needs a rest. I'm not saying it should go away forever. I'm just saying that between Russell's Reserve Single Barrel and Wild Turkey 101, it's not standing as proudly as it has in years gone by. Sure, I've found some quality Kentucky Spirit releases over the last couple of years, but overall, you'll have to agree that the label's seen better days.

But remember, it doesn't have to go away forever. Consider this process:

1. First, mothball the Kentucky Spirit label. Put it to bed and close the door.
2. Next, add a second barrel-entry proof of 107. In other words, keep the current 115 barrel-entry proof, as I feel it's perfect for Russell's Reserve Single Barrel, yet simultaneously age barrels filled at 107

proof. Essentially, you'd have two entirely different Wild Turkey bourbon whiskeys prior to bottle proof.

3. And finally, having reached ideal maturation (presuming eight years), pull those 107 entry-proof barrels, and resurrect Wild Turkey Kentucky Spirit in the form of Jimmy Russell's classic 101-proof, single-barrel bourbon from his classic 107 barrel-entry proof. And a bonus? Bottle it without chill filtration.

How *Will* It Be?

At the end of the day, these are just ideas. I could be completely wrong about Kentucky Spirit's future. Honestly, there's a big part of me that hopes I am. Maybe there's a place for it as-is? Surely there's choice bourbon barrels that fall below 110 proof, making them ineligible for Russell's Reserve Single Barrel. Probably not many, but possibly enough to warrant keeping Kentucky Spirit around. And then there's the recent wave of Camp Nelson barrels, which I've found handle dilution notably well. It's possible those, and other uniquely profiled barrels, justify the need for a continued Kentucky Spirit. Maybe.

In closing, I'd like to stress that I've given this matter a great deal of thought. Probably more than I should've. I've consulted with bourbon friends and fellow Wild Turkey fans alike. There's no single solution we can all agree on. What we do agree on, however, is that the future of Wild Turkey Kentucky Spirit is shaky at best. Something has to change and soon. Whatever that change might be, let's make it count. Let's do it right. No compromises. No apologies.

CAMPARI WHISKEY BARONS: W.B. SAFFELL

Campari Whiskey Barons:
W.B. Saffell

Some whiskeys catch you by complete surprise. It's fair to say W.B. Saffell excelled at that feat. While I'd heard good things from Wild Turkey brand ambassadors in late 2018, I simply chalked it up as employees doing their job. Turns out they were right!

W.B. Saffell was more than a surprising bourbon; it was precisely what Campari's Whiskey Barons series needed. It also couldn't have come at a better time. Considering most special edition bourbons arrive in the fall, an early 2019 release afforded W.B. Saffell the opportunity to attract attention. Granted, it had to overcome the lackluster performance of its forebears in the Whiskey Barons series, which it did.

I suppose the moral of the story is: Eddie Russell makes a difference. dj

FEBRUARY 26, 2019

Campari's Whiskey Barons Collection made its debut in the Spring of 2017. From the beginning there was an air of mystery surrounding the first two releases, Old Ripy and Bond & Lillard. The primary source of confusion was (ironically) the press release, which stated neither Jimmy

Russell nor Eddie Russell was involved with the two expressions, while simultaneously asserting both whiskeys were distilled at Wild Turkey in Lawrenceburg, Kentucky. I guess it depends on what your definition of "involved" is, but for the seasoned enthusiast, the press release created more questions than answers.

Regardless of Old Ripy and Bond & Lillard's origins, the expressions were rather average in the end—neither offensive, nor entirely impressive. While aesthetically beautiful, their stellar designs simply weren't enough to justify their hefty price tag of $50 per 375ml. As such, their popularity and performance were arguably lackluster, each failing to garner the same level of praise given to several contemporary Wild Turkey expressions of comparable specs. In fact, some enthusiasts questioned if the Whiskey Barons program would even continue.

Fast forward one year. In March 2018, the label for W.B. Saffell Bourbon Whiskey hit the TTB COLA registry. Apparently, Campari hadn't thrown in the towel on the Whiskey Barons Collection. And there was even better news this time around: Eddie Russell would be key in crafting Whiskey Baron expressions moving forward. Based on Eddie's track record of exemplary whiskeys (with both Russell's Reserve and Master's Keep), W.B. Saffell seemed promising. If there were ever a chance for the Whiskey Barons Collection to resonate among enthusiasts, it was now or never.

Here we are in 2019, and resting in my hand is a bottle of W.B. Saffell Bourbon Whiskey: Eddie Russell's unique creation, for better or worse. Yet unknown to most, there's a deeper connection surrounding this release. I recently learned that Eddie and family lived in the Saffell house for several years. The late Victorian-era structure is now a funeral home, which in many ways serves as a museum to the once prominent pre-Prohibition distiller. But who was W.B. Saffell and what was his significance to Lawrenceburg?

William Butler Saffell (1843–1910) came to fame in the late nineteenth century. Having worked for distinguished distiller, judge, and politician W.H. McBrayer for some twenty years, Saffell decided to start his own distillery in 1889, the year following McBrayer's death. Despite Saffell's relatively unknown name today, he was considerably successful up until the day he died in 1910 (his impressive home stands as evidence of such). His famous "Sour Mash Kentucky Whiskey" was popular well past his death, rivaling brands like Cedar Brook, the very bourbon Saffell helped

HISTORY ASIDE, I HAVE A JOB TO DO. THE BEST PART IS IT INVOLVES SIPPING WHISKEY.

to put on the map for McBrayer. The W.B. Saffell distillery continued until Prohibition, when its doors closed forever. The Saffell Distillery, its buildings, and brand were eventually lost to time.

I'll happily admit that I'm quite pleased Campari is bringing attention to these lost Lawrenceburg bourbon brands. Sure, it's for a profit (it's a business after all), but they didn't have to choose this route. Thankfully, they did, and (spoiler) after this expression, folks might start paying attention.

The history of Lawrenceburg's distilling past is ripe for the curious mind. While other Kentucky locales gather far greater attention, none seem as unharvested and plentiful as Lawrenceburg's. There's a book-worth there, and someone should write it.

History aside, I have a job to do. The best part is it involves sipping whiskey. While I thoroughly enjoy the nerdy stuff (really, I do), I like the appreciation part a pinch more. And with that, let's see what W.B. Saffell has to offer. It's time for a pour!

Campari Whiskey Barons: W.B. Saffell Batch #1

SPIRIT:	Kentucky straight bourbon whiskey
PROOF:	107
AGE:	not stated (reportedly a blend of six- to twelve-year bourbon)
MISC.:	distilled and bottled by The American Medicinal Spirits Co. (produced at the Wild Turkey Distillery), Lawrenceburg, KY
	tasted neat in a Glencairn Glass after a few minutes rest...
COLOR:	deep copper
NOSE:	(rich and robust) burnt caramel, vanilla bean, molasses, charred oak, brown sugar, clove, blood orange, nutmeg, cinnamon, hints of sweet and savory herbal spice
TASTE:	(notably balanced) vanilla extract, caramel chews, maple syrup, sweet oak char, pecan glaze, ginger beer, pepper, brown sugar, apple peel, nutmeg, faint leather
FINISH:	long, warm and flavorful—toasted vanilla, caramel, sweet and spicy oak, maple, black pepper, clove, licorice, leather, hints of citrus, cinnamon, and sweet herbs

OVERALL:

I have no idea what pre-Prohibition Saffell whiskey tasted like, but if William Butler Saffell could somehow taste this bourbon today, I'd wager he'd be damn proud. This is fantastic... simply fantastic.

I can't say for certain what barrels went into this expression, but I can say there's a strong Camp Nelson vibe at play. Yet, unlike the numerous Camp Nelson rickhouse A and F private selections out there (most of which range eight to nine years), W.B. Saffell has a complex structure with noteworthy maturity. Even at 107 proof, it's unmistakably better than every 110-proof Camp Nelson Russell's Reserve private barrel I've tasted to date.

But of course, there's the elephant in the room. W.B. Saffell's price of $50 for a 375ml non-age-stated bourbon is undoubtedly a significant expense; however, the grand majority of 750ml limited-edition whiskeys often start at well over $100. If Saffell were Old Ripy or Bond & Lillard 1, I'd say try before you buy or simply move along. Luckily, Saffell stands above its preceding Whiskey Baron releases in both proof and profile. Its robust layers and considerable depth remind me of Russell's Reserve 2002, and there's not a single drop of 2002's oaky bitterness.

As far as I'm concerned, W.B. Saffell has earned the title of "2002 Junior." Just think about it: Russell's Reserve 2002 retails for $250. You can throw specs at me all day and tell me why, on paper, Russell's Reserve 2002 is best, etc. Fine. All I have to say in return is that W.B. Saffell deserves similar attention based strictly on profile and personal satisfaction. Yes, it's that good.

Eddie, this should've had a turkey on it.

Campari, Eddie deserves a raise.

In the Presence of Greatness

My first visit to Kentucky was magical, but my first visit to Wild Turkey was life-changing. I returned home in the early morning hours of May 7, 2019. I fashioned myself a quick snack and tried to catch some sleep, but my thoughts kept racing. What an adventure I'd experienced!

Later that day (exhaustion be damned), I sat down to write this blog post. It's one of the few posts I've written in a single session. I had so many details to share, so many emotions to express, it felt as if my fingers couldn't type fast enough. By the time I'd finished, I'd lived the experience all over again (and finished a few Turkeys in the process). dj

MAY 7, 2019

The past two days are days I'll never forget.

I left my home in South Carolina not quite knowing what was ahead of me. Of course, one always has visions of what things will be like— conversations and moments you'll possibly share with others, how people and places will look and sound; mental expectations, if you will. I had all of these things swirling in my head as I boarded the plane bound for Lexington, Kentucky. Little did I know that my dreams would be exceeded in virtually every way.

As my flight approached the LEX runway, I was captivated by the landscape below me. You hear folks talk about hills of bluegrass and picturesque farmland as if those are unique. They are. Kentucky is beautiful. I stepped off the plane, and just paces away, in the airport no less, I found my first bourbon shop. Its shelves were lined with bottles I rarely find in Carolina. Yet as tempting as it was to grab an early souvenir, I had far greater things ahead of me.

REMEMBER WHEN YOU WERE A KID AND YOU HAD TROUBLE FALLING ASLEEP CHRISTMAS EVE? WELL, THAT WAS MY SLEEP SUNDAY EVENING.

After a brief time in my hotel (thank you, Residence Inn Keeneland, for the excellent service) and a much-needed chat with my family, I met up with two bourbon amigos I've talked with many times online but never met in person: Scott Early and Ryan Alves. I ran into Scott first, as he was staying in the same hotel. We shared a pour of a damn-fine Russell's Reserve Single Barrel Bourbon, the 2018 Kentucky Bourbon Affair Legend's Select (thank you very much, Scott). Shortly after, Scott and I were met by Ryan, and we headed off to my first annual gathering for Patreon supporters. After a quick stop at Red State BBQ to pick up dinner for the get together, we made it to Base 110 in downtown Lexington. (Both Red State and Base 110 get my highest recommendations, by the way.)

As Scott and Ryan were setting up, I spent a little time recording an episode for The Bourbon Road podcast. Thanks to Jim and Randy for their kindness and professionalism.

And the gathering commenced . . .

Words can't describe the appreciation I have for the individuals who support my blog through Patreon each month. Sunday was my chance to give back, both in passion and in person. We sipped epic pours, shared incredible conversations, and most importantly, we did it all through a bond forged by Wild Turkey. A few lucky folks left with prizes, including a spot on our Wild Turkey barrel pick the following day (congrats, Jon). Special thanks to Brad for donating a 2007 Wild Turkey 101 and to Mikey for throwing in a Wild Turkey ball cap (you both made two attendees very happy). An esteemed guest was also in attendance: Brian Haara, author of *Bourbon Justice*. Brian signed books and contributed to the door prizes as well (thank you, Brian). It was a night I'll never forget, especially that 2001 Rare Breed Batch 01-99 (wowzah!).

Back at the hotel, I had a hard time catching sleep. The excitement of the gathering took some time to settle down. I also missed my family back in South Carolina, but I needed to stay focused and get good rest. The day ahead was a big one. I was going to "The House that Jimmy Built."

Remember when you were a kid and you had trouble falling asleep Christmas Eve? Well, that was my sleep Sunday evening. Nevertheless, I awoke Monday morning fueled by anticipation and excitement. After quickly getting ready, I found a few minutes to sit down for a nice complimentary breakfast at the hotel with Scott and another bourbon friend, Kevin Williams. I should mention that Kevin had some very entertaining stories to tell throughout the trip. His presence really gave my visit an authentic Kentucky charm, and I'd like to say thanks to him for that.

After a half-hour or so on the road, we approached Wild Turkey. Crossing over the Kentucky River and seeing the distillery on the hill, I felt as if I'd entered a world all its own. For those that have never been, Wild Turkey is

everything and nothing like you'd imagine. It's gorgeous and timeless, but it's not fancy. It's simple yet enriched with a history that shows in its grounds. Even the newest buildings feel like they've been there for ages. The landscape is strikingly natural—almost untouched by man. You hear wildlife. You feel the sun. And despite being yards from a large operating distillery, you breathe fresh air. As I said, everything and nothing like you'd imagine.

As we approached the visitors center, the "Cathedral to Bourbon," as it's appropriately called, there was electricity within our group. While we all came from different places, different trades, and different walks of life, we all shared a love for Wild Turkey. You could feel it from the first minute our feet hit the ground. Everything was perfect. There was no doubt in our minds, this would be a special day.

Before getting started on the distillery tour and barrel selection, I took a few minutes to browse the visitors center alone. I met and talked with some wonderful and kind employees of Wild Turkey—folks like Bo Garrett and Allison Pinkston, who excel at making you feel welcome. I reviewed the wall of Wild Turkey's history, learning a few new things (and finding one or two trivial inaccuracies). And then, Eddie and Bruce Russell walked in.

If you've ever had the pleasure of meeting Eddie Russell, you know that he takes his job seriously. After a minute or two saying good morning to our group, he and Bruce were off to Warehouse A. After all, there were barrels to be picked and people waiting to pick them. We'd see a lot more of Eddie and Bruce later.

Just as Eddie left, JoAnn Street, Eddie's niece, introduced herself and led us to a bus for a short ride to an in-depth tour of the distillery situated on the hill above the visitors center. JoAnn did a fantastic job. She was knowledgeable and patient and added notable energy to topics that many wouldn't necessarily find thrilling. As you'd probably guess, there's a mountain of science and complex machinery behind a modern distillery. JoAnn made it sound easy, accessible, and relatable. It was an informative tour that frankly couldn't have been any better.

And then it was time to meet Eddie and Bruce at Warehouse A for our barrel selection. Riding by all of the rickhouses on the way to A was surreal. I realized I was passing hundreds of barrels that I'd one day be sipping whiskey from, be it in batches or as single barrels. Literally living history, crafted from hard work and slowly aging in American Oak. As I said, surreal.

We arrived at Warehouse A and were met by a new friend and stellar photographer, Victor Sizemore. Victor had started his morning shooting pictures for my upcoming book and was now joining us for the barrel selection. Soon after, Bruce arrived, and we all talked on the rickhouse porch for a few minutes as Eddie was finishing a barrel selection with another group.

Eddie wrapped up and stepped out of the rickhouse door ready to go. Armed only with an old copper thief, a well-used hammer, and a leather-bound notebook, he guided us into the rickhouse. And the smell . . . whiskey and wood blended in an almost indescribable "ancient" scent. It was cool, with an odd touch of moisture, yet enticing and relaxing at the same time. Truthfully, it's the kind of place I'd love to hang a hammock.

I thought about the history of the rickhouse, built in 1894. Its floors were once walked by James P. Ripy and his four nephews, who started Ripy Brothers Distillery; Jimmy Russell's mentor, Master Distiller Bill Hughes; countless employees and guests for well over a century; and every Russell who ever worked at Wild Turkey. And here we were . . . walking those very same floors.

With copitas and water bottles in hand, Eddie started popping the bungs and filling our glasses. Barrel after barrel we tasted, each one with contemplation and joy. There wasn't a bad one in the bunch (didn't expect there to be), but with so many quality choices, you have to make hard decisions. But who's complaining? We narrowed it down to four, three of which were fairly close in profile. At that point, we decided to re-taste blind, so Bruce and JoAnn set that up for us. We again tasted, and the choices were unanimous: two barrels from Camp Nelson's rickhouse F. Beasts of barrels, I must say.

We finished up the blind samples and moved on to tasting two remarkable rye barrels, both personal favorites of Bruce Russell. One was pure bubblegum, and if I could've taken that barrel home, I damn sure would've! Per Bruce, these were barrels originally destined for the upcoming Master's Keep Cornerstone, but either by chance or circumstance, they remained in rickhouse A. Lucky us! It seemed at that point things were winding down, that is until we were drawn to the "truck barrel."

Earlier in our selection process, an employee walked into the rickhouse and notified Eddie a truck was outside with more barrels. As it turns out, the entire load of the 18-wheeler trailer was a single barrel. It was just sitting there . . . all alone and begging to be tapped. We all laughed about it yet felt compelled to ask Eddie about making a tasting happen. Thankfully, he did. We each jumped into the trailer and tasted the barrel. It was a rock-solid Turkey profile—"classically modern," you might say. My guess was Camp Nelson A, and it turned out to be just that. On the spot, Adam Howard, the sponsoring vendor, and manager of Lexington Beverage Outlet, decided a third barrel would be purchased. The "truck barrel" would forever be known as "Swan Song: A Barrel to Remember."

All in all, we tasted eleven barrels (fifteen if you count the blind tasting). As you can imagine, we were in need of sustenance, so we said our good-byes to Eddie, JoAnn, and Warehouse A and headed to Heavens to Betsy in downtown Lawrenceburg. Bruce joined us for a friendly lunch of great food, great company, and great conversation. He informed us that Jimmy would be waiting for us back at the visitors center, so with full bellies, we made our way back to Wild Turkey to see the man himself.

I want to pause for a moment and say that Jimmy Russell is a national treasure. He is the last of his kind: a master distiller's master distiller. If you ever have the chance to talk with him, please do. As stubborn as they say Jimmy might be on the job, he is more than personable, patient, and gracious with his customers and fans. He is a true rarity.

One by one, we all took our time with Jimmy. He told stories about the old times, signed bottles, cut jokes, and made us feel right at home. And then I had the chance to speak with Jimmy one on one. Half an hour seemed like five minutes. I didn't want it to end. Unfortunately, there were others waiting, so I said my goodbyes and thanked Jimmy.

I decided I'd spend my last few minutes in the gift shop, thinking I'd find something small enough for the flight home. I browsed the selection and chatted with a few bourbon friends in the process, all down-to-Earth folks like Scott Forosisky and his good friend, Nellie Kuh, who were so positive to be around. That's when I looked over my shoulder to see Jimmy sitting alone at the table. He motioned to me. "Come back over," he said with a smile and waved me to the table. I sat back down, childish grin and all. We talked more about the old times. I asked him about Master Distiller Bill Hughes, and he told me about the day Hughes suffered a stroke in the distillery. Jimmy said they had to carry him out, and he seemed to recall it as if it happened yesterday. We talked about Booker Noe and Elmer T. Lee's importance, as well as Parker Beam's courageous battle with Amyotrophic Lateral Sclerosis (ALS). Every word from Jimmy was from the heart. It was just as the words embossed on Wild Turkey bottles read: Bold. Genuine. True. That's Jimmy Russell to me.

I said farewell to Jimmy, Bruce, JoAnn, and all of the fine folks at the distillery and headed out with my friend T.J. Thompson, proprietor of Thompson Woodworks, and his wife, Nikki, for one last bite to eat and a sip or two with Victor Sizemore at Goodfellas in Lexington. Operating out of the original James E. Pepper Distillery, Goodfellas is the kind of place I wish I had in my hometown. The atmosphere, food, and drinks were perfect, as was the service. I enjoyed a well-crafted Rittenhouse Rye Old Fashioned, a tasty five-year Willett Single Barrel, and a sip of the new Jim Beam Legent (it's no Master's Keep Revival—apologies, Fred Noe). But just when I thought my day was done, Victor invited us to an Old Carter Whiskey Co. tasting at Justins' House of Bourbon. I'm so glad he did.

At Justins', I met and talked at length with Mark and Sherri Carter. We tasted four barrel-strength rye whiskeys, one barrel-strength bourbon, and one twenty-seven-year American whiskey (likely Seagram's)—all blends of around five to thirteen barrels each. I'll have to admit, they were incredibly delicious. Say what you will about sourced whiskey, but the rye bottles were undeniably impressive. There's just something about a well-aged, barrel-proof 95% rye mash bill whiskey that explodes in your mouth like a never-ending flavor bomb. And Mark and Sherri were both so pleasant to talk with, both full of enthusiasm and open to our honest opinions. I genuinely appreciate their hospitality.

With a long and wondrous day behind me, T.J. and Nikki kindly drove me to the airport. With goodbyes exchanged, I walked into the terminal with a huge smile of satisfaction on my face. Since the moment my plane landed the day before, I'd been in the presence of greatness. A truly beautiful state, a memorable evening with friends and supporters over cherished pours, a visit to the best distillery in the world, amazing whiskey tasted straight from the barrel, precious time with the Russells, food and fellowship with friends old and new . . . greatness was all around me.

I'm so very grateful to everyone that made this trip so special. I'll never forget these past two days, and I look forward to my next visit with eager joy. And to Jimmy Russell, thank you for taking the time to talk with me and for making Wild Turkey what it is today.

WHAT'S A DUSTY?

What's a Dusty?

There are a great number of words in the English language that lack precise definition. How many grains of sand constitute a pile? What about a mound? The same concept applies to certain terms used in whiskey enthusiasm.

Take the word "dusty," for example. At what point in time does a whiskey release achieve dusty status? How about a Wild Turkey release? After a barrage of email inquiries and social media messages asking for assistance with various dusty finds, I felt compelled to clarify—or attempt to clarify—how the word dusty applies to Wild Turkey. Of course, it wasn't easy. dj

JUNE 11, 2019

You see it all the time, the word "dusty." What's a dusty? You might know already (or think you know), but do you? How does one really know when a bourbon is a dusty? How about a dusty Wild Turkey? Are they the same? Are they worth more? Do they taste better? If I have a dusty that has no dust on it, is it still a dusty? All good questions. Let's explore these today, shall we?

If you're new to whiskey enthusiasm, bourbons referred to as "dusty" are older releases still found sitting on retail shelves; in other words, older bottles found literally collecting dust. There are no hard rules as to what defines a bourbon as dusty (it's quite subjective, honestly), but when you hear the word, it frequently (if not always) infers a desirable or choice find.

Alright, I'm just going to bust out of the gates and say it—a "transitional label" (2011–2015) Wild Turkey 101 bottle isn't a dusty, at least not yet. It's a retired label, sure. It may have actual dust on it, and the words "Austin, Nichols" (I'll give it that), but a dusty it ain't. Or maybe you've recently "hit the jackpot" with an entire shelf of Rare Breed batch 112.8! Yeah, no. That's not a dusty. Sorry. Ah, but Rare Breed batch 03RB . . . that's dusty, right? Ehh, maybe. But let's stop right there and take a step back. Don't worry. I'll circle back to Rare Breed 03RB.

Whiskey, like so many other hobbies, has its share of vocabulary with seemingly unknown origins. "Shelf turd," "unicorn," "tater," "dusty" . . . we see these every day, yet their backstories are hazy at best. So, when did the word "dusty" enter the whiskey lexicon? It's hard to say for sure, but my best guess would be early to mid-2000s. Why? The internet was experiencing rapid growth, and bourbon was once again gaining in popularity. Folks from around the world could now communicate with one another easily and instantaneously. Descriptors developed just as rapidly. For example, I was into coin collecting at that time, and though words like "gems" and "culls" were likely used prior to the internet, they really took off afterwards. The same goes for whiskey words. Terms like "dusty" were probably spoken well before they were typed; nevertheless, they didn't become part of the hobby-wide vernacular until the internet arrived. At least, that's my hypothesis.

So, what constitutes a dusty in terms of whiskey, more specifically in terms of Wild Turkey? There are only two guidelines I use for determining "dusty" Turkey:

1. The release date of the bottle.
2. Its overall flavor profile.

DATING DUSTY

Let's start with my first guideline, release date. When it comes to Wild Turkey, I usually default to the ten-year rule. That being, if a bottle (not the whiskey itself) isn't at least ten years old, it's not considered dusty. Does that apply universally to all American whiskey labels? No. For example, Elijah Craig 12-Year (particularly with the red "12" on the front label) might be considered a dusty, as it's been discontinued (redesigned and reformulated) for several years now and remains remarkably popular. I'm not saying it's worth a premium (I was never a fan of the twelve-year Elijah Craig), I'm just saying that calling it a dusty is arguably acceptable at this point, even though it's been less than ten years since its age statement was dropped.

As for Wild Turkey, any of its straight whiskey expressions sitting on a retail shelf since 2009 or earlier, I think it's reasonable to call that a dusty in today's bourbon-hype environment. Note that I said "straight whiskey." Finding a 2009 American Honey liqueur isn't exactly something to jump up and down about. Sure, you can call that a dusty if you want to. Just don't expect a lot of high fives from bourbon geeks or likes on your social media posts. But let's say you find a Kentucky Spirit from 2008. Sure, that's possibly a dusty Turkey, and a great find in my opinion. Same for a 2006 Wild Turkey 101 or a 2007 Russell's Reserve 6-Year Rye, etc.

But it's not just the release date alone that matters, it's the profile, too. I can't speak for every bourbon label out there, but when it comes to Wild Turkey, the releases I consider dusty should have a profile to match the designation. This is where things get a little tricky, as subjectivity plays a large role.

Tasting Dusty

Some years back, I created a Wild Turkey Bourbon Profile chart. While it's far from perfect, it was my attempt to illustrate how Wild Turkey from different eras taste. At first glance, it appears chronological; however, note that the interlocking circles mean you'll often have profile crossover. In other words, a 2019 Russell's Reserve Single Barrel Bourbon might have some throwback classic character to it. Alternatively, a 2004 Wild Turkey 101 might have some dusty notes, while a 1993 Wild Turkey 101 some classic notes. Again, the chart is imperfect, but it's my best effort at describing how older Wild Turkey releases can taste.

WILD TURKEY BOURBON PROFILES

"DUSTY"
- FLORAL PERFUME
- SWEET HERBS & SPICE
- FRAGRANT TOBACCO
- LEATHER

"CLASSIC"
- RICH VANILLA
- HONEY–MAPLE
- BROWN SUGAR
- MUSTY OAK

"MODERN"
- "NUTTY" TOFFEE
- CARAMEL
- BAKING SPICE
- SLIGHTLY "GRAINY"

What accounts for these differences in flavor profiles? After all, Jimmy Russell has said time and time again that nothing has changed. This is an article-worthy topic in and of itself, but let me make something clear: Jimmy Russell means what he says (and says exactly what he means). Sure, Wild Turkey's facilities have seen upgrades, and were completely rebuilt by 2011. There are steel fermentation tanks instead of cypress wood, not to mention a brand new still and computers running it all. The barrel-entry proof has changed, twice. But these are equipment and operational changes.

When Jimmy says nothing has changed, he means the method in which the bourbon is crafted—its recipe, yeast, fermentation time (by smell and taste), barrel char, how it's evaluated, etc. The way former master distillers Bill Hughes and Ernie Ripy taught Jimmy to make bourbon, that's how Jimmy taught Eddie. To Jimmy, nothing has changed. If a chef cooks the same recipe in two different pans on two different stoves, would you classify the end result as two different dishes? I don't think so.

Nevertheless, Wild Turkey's overall flavor profile has changed over the years. Hell, the flavor profiles for all long-standing bourbon brands have changed. It's not a phenomenon unique to Wild Turkey. There are countless reasons for this, and Michael Veach's article, "Old Bottle Bourbon Flavor," does an excellent job explaining why (a highly recommended read, by the way). My point is, Wild Turkey isn't the same Wild Turkey any more than Jim Beam isn't the same Jim Beam or Maker's Mark isn't the same Maker's Mark.

DETERMINING DUSTY

As for how this all relates to the word dusty, I think it's imperative that one takes into consideration both the age of the bottle itself and its whiskey's flavor profile. I'll use Wild Turkey Rare Breed batch 03RB as an example.

Let's say you find a bottle of Rare Breed batch 03RB. Is that a dusty? Maybe. Batch 03RB has the unique distinction of being the longest-produced

WILD TURKEY'S OVERALL FLAVOR PROFILE HAS CHANGED OVER THE YEARS

Rare Breed batch to date, filling bottles from roughly 2004 to 2013. Does every bottle of Rare Breed 03RB taste the same? With the exception of black plastic wrap in 2004, they certainly look the same. Unfortunately (or fortunately, depending on personal preference), they don't taste the same: 2004 03RB tastes closer to Rare Breed batch 01-99, while 2013 03RB doesn't really taste like 2004 03RB or 2014's batch 112.8 either.

To me, earlier bottles of Rare Breed 03RB are richer in classic notes, arguably some dusty notes buried within. Conversely, latter 03RB batches have what I'd classify as a combination of classic and modern notes. Most of these variances between 2004–2013 Rare Breed bottles have to do with barrel-entry proof changes, as 2004 would've been batched from whiskey barreled at 107 proof, while 2013 03RB batched from whiskey barreled at 107, 110, and 115. But then, different rickhouses are in season every year (each with their own profile traits), so simple batch variance shouldn't be understated either. While Jimmy and Eddie do a great job of achieving batch consistency year to year, finding consistency from today to nine years back is arguably tough.

But back to the question of whether Rare Breed 03RB is a dusty find. Well, I'd say it depends on the bottle's year. A black-wrap 2004 Rare Breed

03RB is a true dusty find, in my opinion. A 2013 03RB . . . not so much. Sure, it's a cool Austin, Nichols label, but it's not really a dusty bourbon. Five years from now, I might (and probably will) tell you differently. As for today, I'd say the last two years of 03RB contain enough modern notes to dispute calling them dusty. But as mentioned earlier, it's all subjective. You're free to call it a dusty all day long. Just don't expect universal acceptance in doing so.

So, why does any of this matter? What's the purpose of this article? It's pretty simple, actually. Money. The secondary market value for Wild Turkey expressions has increased substantially over the past two years. Bottles are selling for higher than ever before, and the word "dusty" helps to drive those values. If you're relatively new to bourbon enthusiasm and actively seeking vintage bottles, particularly Wild Turkey, be careful. Just because something is labeled "dusty Turkey," that doesn't mean it's worth a premium. In fact, many bottles that folks tout as dusty can frequently be found on shelves. There's no need to spend extra hard-earned money on everyday retail finds. Be mindful, do your research, and never take the word "dusty" for granted.

Cheers and happy hunting!

ASTER'S KEEP

UCKY STRAIG

WHIS

54.5% ALC/VOL (109 PROOF)

CRAFTED *with* CONVICTION

WILD TURKEY®

KENTUCKY STRAIGHT RYE WHISKEY

— CORNERSTONE —

WILD TURKEY
MASTER'S KEEP
CORNERSTONE

Wild Turkey Master's Keep Cornerstone

I was excited beyond words when I first learned Wild
Turkey was releasing a limited-edition rye whiskey.
Since the earliest days of my Wild Turkey fandom, I'd
always felt that rye was an area of tremendous potential
for the brand. Having tasted rye whiskey straight from
the barrel in Lawrenceburg, I still feel that way (and
probably will for the rest of my life).

When the time came to review Master's Keep Cornerstone,
I knew it was best to focus on the significance of the
release just as much, if not more, than the whiskey
itself. More importantly, it was an appropriate time to
shine a light on the contributions of Bruce Russell. His
name may not grace the bottle or box, but his influence
is evident in the spirit. dj

AUGUST 13, 2019

cor·ner·stone

/'kôrnər,stōn/

noun

1. An important quality or feature on which a particular thing depends
    or is based. (*Oxford Lexico*)

W hen most people hear the words "Wild Turkey," they think bourbon. And rightfully so, as Jimmy Russell's incomparable Kentucky straight bourbon whiskey has been filling glasses and satisfying souls for scores of years. Yet, from the very beginning, going back before the Russell era, Wild Turkey rye whiskey stocked retail shelves.

I've discussed the history of Wild Turkey rye before, most recently in my review of a 2018 81-proof Wild Turkey Straight Rye. Essentially, Wild Turkey 101 Rye, just like the bourbon, began with sourced whiskey. It wasn't until the 1970s, after the purchase of (what's now) the Wild Turkey distillery by Austin, Nichols & Co., that rye whiskey distillation began under Jimmy Russell's supervision in Lawrenceburg, Kentucky.

But here's the kicker: Jimmy Russell isn't a rye whiskey fan. Sure, he knows how to craft it, but you won't find him sipping it in his leisure time. And there's nothing wrong with that. You like what you like. At the same time, Jimmy's preference for bourbon (and lack of consumer rye demand for decades) is probably why we've never seen a special-edition Wild Turkey rye whiskey. That is, until 2019.

Whiskey enthusiasts have known about Master's Keep Cornerstone since late 2018. Immediately, the energy was high for this release. Wild Turkey's first limited edition straight rye whiskey—its longest aged and highest proof—would soon be in the hands of fans. With an official release date set for August 2019, it came as a surprise when bottles popped up in several states a month early. And then, the mania hit. With only 16,000 bottles available domestically (6,000 internationally), and considering the attention limited whiskey releases get nowadays (Google "whiskey tater"), the chances of acquiring Cornerstone seemed slimmer by the day.

But hold up. We are talking about Wild Turkey rye, right? Not Sazerac 18, not Van Winkle Family Reserve Rye, not some insanely priced, pewter-top WhistlePig luxury bottle, no. Wild Turkey rye (the same Wild Turkey rye we've known for years now) is finally getting the attention it deserves. How about that!

So, who's to thank for this endeavor? Well, that would be Master Distiller Eddie Russell and his son, Global Brand Ambassador Bruce Russell. Though as much as Cornerstone bears Eddie's name, the unsung hero of this special release is undoubtedly Bruce.

Bruce Russell is in every way the modern steward of Wild Turkey rye. Without Bruce, Master's Keep Cornerstone likely wouldn't exist. I think both Jimmy and Eddie Russell would agree with that statement. It takes passion to make something truly extraordinary. While Jimmy has always produced excellent rye whiskey, he's never put it forth as a special limited expression. To do so might appear disingenuous, and that sure as hell ain't Jimmy Russell. But as Bruce came of age, he shared his passion for rye whiskey with his father, Eddie, and Eddie took note.

Much like Jimmy, Eddie went for years with minimal appreciation for rye. Bruce, through his focus and zeal, changed Eddie's perspective. Rye whiskey became more than a supplementary product: it became a show-piece for the Russell's Reserve brand, as evidenced by its launch of Russell's Reserve Single Barrel Rye in 2015. But little did we know that Eddie and Bruce were just getting started.

Master's Keep Cornerstone is exactly what its name implies: an import-ant basis cemented in the past and present—the start of a new foundation with limitless potential. I have a lot to say about Cornerstone, though I'm struggling to do so in my usual format. So today, I'll be changing things up a bit. I'll start with the specs, as I always do, but instead of simply listing notes for each phase of the tasting, I'll also provide my thoughts in detail from phase to phase. I'm not certain it'll be a format I'll continue for future reviews, but it's certainly warranted for this occasion. So, with that, let's pour!

Wild Turkey Master's Keep Cornerstone

SPIRIT:	Kentucky straight rye whiskey
PROOF:	109
AGE:	nine to eleven years
MISC.:	bottled by Wild Turkey Distilling Co., Lawrenceburg, KY; batch #0001 bottle #22752
	tasted neat in a Glencairn Glass after a few minutes rest…
COLOR:	rich copper
NOSE:	graham crackers, medicinal cherry, vanilla wafers, baked apples, oak, pepper, lemon squares, ginger, red grapefruit, herbal spice, brown sugar glaze, faint sweet dough

With the exception of some additional spice, oak, and red fruit, Cornerstone's nose is very much in line with Russell's Reserve Single Barrel Rye. The medicinal cherry note—one that first struck me on my recent livestream with Jason Callori. of The Mash & Drum—is unique among the modern Wild Turkey rye expressions I've tasted. Outside of those attributes, you'll find the typical vanilla, lemon squares, sweet herbs, and ginger often found in Wild Turkey rye whiskey. An enjoyable nose, though I wouldn't consider it the highlight of this expression.

And the ride intensifies…

TASTE:	(notably spicy and textured) pepper, apples and cinnamon, clove, old-fashioned caramel chews, black tea, blood orange, floral honey, licorice, lemon-vanilla, oak char, hints of cherry

The pepper one discovers upon nosing transitions into a full-force dominant note by the time this whiskey hits the palate. But pepper isn't the only presence making itself known; there's plenty of spice and sweetness— virtually sparring—on your tongue. You feel it as you taste it, but it's only a tease of what's to come with the finish. As for the mouthfeel, I wouldn't necessarily call it thick in the creamy, buttery sense (that's Russell's Reserve Single Barrel Rye), but more textured and tactile, endowed with the signature "Camp Nelson prickle."

And now, the pièce de résistance . . .

FINISH: remarkably long and peppery—black pepper, sweet chiles, vanilla spice, dense charred oak, licorice, leather, Coca-Cola Classic, citrus zest, confectioner sugar, ginger beer, lingering cinnamon and clove

What an excellent finish! Waves of black pepper intertwine with charred oak and sweet cola in a seemingly never-ending medley of complexity and maturity. I've experienced lengthy finishes before but never from a Wild Turkey rye expression—not like this. There's a lot going on here, and it's not just earth and spice. There's intense vanilla, zesty citrus, and a sly, sugary lace that weaves through layers of licorice and faint ginger beer. By far, the finish is the premier aspect of this whiskey, an aspect that sets it apart from numerous Kentucky straight rye whiskeys of practically every price tier.

OVERALL:

What can I say? Master's Keep Cornerstone is the best modern Wild Turkey rye whiskey expression I've had to date. It's a high-quality pour, but it's not the end-all, be-all of Wild Turkey limited editions—not even close. Don't get me wrong. Cornerstone has a lot to offer the Wild Turkey and rye whiskey enthusiast. At the same time, it touts a fair share of commonalities with Russell's Reserve Single Barrel Rye, enough to make one weigh the more than $100 price difference between the two. They're not the same, but they're not entirely distant either.

My advice to anyone contemplating the $175 purchase is try before you buy. And if the opportunity presents itself, taste Cornerstone against Russell's Reserve Single Barrel Rye. Hell, throw in a pour of Wild Turkey 101 Rye and Russell's Reserve 6-Year Rye for good measure. Go blind. You might just find your preference leans towards the younger, sweeter profiles of 101 Rye and Russell's Reserve 6-Year. However, if you're a fan of Russell's Reserve Single Barrel Rye but want a little more ABV and significant peppery spice, you'll likely appreciate the investment.

Before signing off, I'd like to say to Eddie Russell, you did a damn fine job with this whiskey, sir. But your work is far from done. I expect even finer limited-edition rye expressions down the road, expressions that will affirm precisely what Cornerstone's name implies—a strong foundation.

And readers, note there's something greater here, a much deeper meaning in this whiskey's name. If you think about it, when filled, the barrels comprising Cornerstone were originally destined for Wild Turkey's standard rye offerings. If it weren't for Bruce Russell, that's all they might've been. Bruce found a level of passion for rye whiskey that was undiscovered by his father and grandfather. He saw something truly special and the promise of what could be.

Ladies and gentlemen, when it comes to the future of Wild Turkey rye, the cornerstone isn't a bottle of whiskey: it's Bruce Cassidy Russell.

WILD TURKEY RYE TIMELINE
(* = APPROXIMATE TIME)

1950*: Wild Turkey 101 Rye sourced from Baltimore Pure Rye in Maryland.

1960*: Wild Turkey 101 Rye sourced from Michter's/Pennco in Pennsylvania: supplementary rye whiskey sourced from Maryland and Illinois (presumed Hiram Walker & Sons) through at least 1979.

1974*: Wild Turkey rye distillation moved to the Austin, Nichols Distillery in Kentucky.

2007: Russell's Reserve 6 Year Old Rye is introduced.

2012: Wild Turkey Rye (81 proof) is introduced; Wild Turkey 101 Rye is allocated to limited distribution.

2013: Wild Turkey Forgiven, a bourbon and rye blend, is released as a limited edition.

2014: Wild Turkey 101 Rye distribution is increased (primarily as liter bottles).

2015: Russell's Reserve Single Barrel Rye is introduced.

2019: Wild Turkey Master's Keep Cornerstone, the brand's first limited edition rye whiskey, is released.

2020: Wild Turkey Rare Breed Rye makes its debut at 112.2 proof (NCF).

THE ESSENCE OF JIMMY RUSSELL

The Essence of Jimmy Russell

I'd been anticipating Jimmy Russell's sixty-fifth anniversary at Wild Turkey for months. My original plan
hinged on timing *American Spirit*'s release to coincide
with the event. *Ha!* I had so much to learn as a new
author (still do).

With a September book release no longer an option, I
endeavored to write a special blog entry for Jimmy's
anniversary. Surely, every other whiskey blogger would
be covering his legendary past. Then it hit me . . . why
not approach the piece from the angle of Jimmy Russell's
contributions to the Wild Turkey brand? I focused on the
expressions that stood the test of time and those which
remain as unique as Jimmy after sixty-five uncompromising years. dj

SEPTEMBER 10, 2019

Today is a special day for Jimmy Russell and Wild Turkey; more importantly, though, a special day for bourbon.

September 10, 2019 marks Master Distiller Jimmy Russell's sixty-fifth anniversary at Wild Turkey Distilling Co. Sixty-five years. Incredible. Who works at the same distillery (or any job, really) for sixty-five years? Almost no one . . . except James Cassidy Russell.

Pardon my French, but Jimmy Russell is a bourbon badass. I don't mean that in a flippant, irreverent sense. Not at all. I mean that in the most earnest sense. Jimmy Russell is a bourbon badass. His experience, mature beyond his years. His humility, as unfiltered as his stubbornness. His skill, as bold and genuine as a straight whiskey gets. Author Fred Minnick once said to me, "Wild Turkey is the quintessential bourbon story." To that I'll add that its indisputable centerpiece is Jimmy Russell. Rock 'n' roll has Elvis. Country has Hank. Soul has Marvin. Bourbon has Jimmy.

You'll likely read a lot about Jimmy over the next few weeks. And you should. After all, Jimmy's sixty-fifth should be celebrated indefinitely as far as I'm concerned. But instead of discussing Jimmy's life and times with bourbon (there'll be plenty of opportunities for that), I'm going to focus on his long-standing contributions to the brand itself . . . "The Essence of Jimmy Russell," if you will.

Imagine our world fifty years from now. Picture a bottle of Wild Turkey bourbon. What do you see? 101, most likely. Or maybe it's Rare Breed or Kentucky Spirit. But, chances are, you're thinking of an expression that wouldn't exist without Jimmy Russell. I know, I know. I hear the comments from the bourbon-geek peanut gallery already. Yes, Wild Turkey 101 existed before Jimmy Russell started distilling bourbon. Just hold your Glencairn. I'll get to that in a bit.

Before getting started, I should say that if you want the real Jimmy Russell experience, head down to Lawrenceburg and meet the man. He's often found "holding court" at the visitors center. He'll happily talk to you for hours. Graciously sign your bottles. Smile affectionately for your photos. Make you laugh. Make you thirsty. That's Jimmy Russell through and through. Hell, it's that exact incomparable warm attitude that arguably saved bourbon from virtual extinction in the 1980s and 1990s. Booker, Elmer, and Parker all played crucial roles, but there's a magnetism surrounding Jimmy you need only experience once, and your life is forever changed.

Jimmy Russell dispels myths, opens minds, and reverses staunch opinions in a matter of minutes armed only with a grin and eighty-four years of honest Kentucky country-boy wisdom. It's not that he's trying to convert you (though he wants you to love bourbon as much as he does); it's not a sales pitch. He wholeheartedly shares his passion with you. And whether you prefer your bourbon neat, on the rocks, in a cocktail, or even as a flavored liqueur, he doesn't fault you for it. He just wants you to love it, in whatever way means most to you.

What if you can't make it to Lawrenceburg? How does one experience the essence of Jimmy Russell? Sure, there's podcasts and YouTube (I highly recommend Al Young's Nunn Center series, as well as the official Diamond Anniversary video), but there's arguably a better way to connect to all that Jimmy has to offer. Ladies and gentlemen, the essence of Jimmy Russell can easily be found in his personally crafted whiskeys. His "bourbon babies," as I like to call them.

On this day of Mr. Russell's astounding sixty-five-year distilling career, I'll count down Jimmy's industry best. No, they're not rare "dusty" bottles. They're not limited editions, export-only curiosities, or collectible ceramic decanters either. They're the expressions that Jimmy's legacy will forever be tied to. Sixty-five years of quality and magic sitting on your local liquor store's shelves.

5. WILD TURKEY AMERICAN HONEY (FORMERLY WILD TURKEY LIQUEUR)

I realize my readership is made up primarily of bourbon enthusiasts, so this particular entry is sure to get some eye-rolls and mumbles. But stick with me.

Did you know that Jimmy Russell invented flavored bourbon? Long before Red Stag and Fireball there was Wild Turkey Liqueur (1976). A simple combination of Wild Turkey bourbon, pure sugar and honey, Wild Turkey Liqueur was Jimmy's way of attracting new consumers at a time when bourbon was far from *en vogue*. Did it work? Well enough that sales of the spirit are still strong today. While known as Wild Turkey American Honey since 2006, the neoclassic liqueur is found virtually everywhere. And personally, combined with an equal part of Wild Turkey 101, there's no better Hot Toddy base out there.

4. RUSSELL'S RESERVE 10 YEAR OLD BOURBON (FORMERLY WILD TURKEY RUSSELL'S RESERVE)

Years before Russell's Reserve was a brand, it was a ten-year, 101-proof Wild Turkey bourbon. The first Wild Turkey domestic release to bear an age statement since the discontinuation of Wild Turkey 101 8-Year and 101

12-Year, Russell's Reserve 10-Year was a welcome expression for veteran Wild Turkey fans in 2001.

In 2005, Russell's Reserve 10-Year was lowered to 90 proof and transitioned to the more familiar squat-sized bottle. Its label and embossing have changed a few times since, most notably the inclusion of Eddie Russell's name as master distiller in 2015, but the whiskey within remains a testament to Jimmy's excellence in crafting mature yet elegant, easily approachable whiskey.

3. WILD TURKEY KENTUCKY SPIRIT

Ancient Age Master Distiller Elmer T. Lee introduced Blanton's to the world in 1984. It was the first mass-market, single-barrel bourbon release, and it debuted at a time when the industry was waist-deep in the infamous "Glut Era." A bold move by Elmer, no doubt.

Whether Jimmy Russell admired his friend's gamble or just thought it was plain crazy, the release ultimately worked, and Jimmy wisely took note. By 1994, the first Wild Turkey Kentucky Spirit bottles were filled, at the brand's signature 101 proof, no less. They were very much a reflection of Blanton's: ornate glass, a hefty pewter top, and handwritten barrel details on each label. Wild Turkey's first single-barrel bourbon expression was a respectable success, quickly earning its status as a staple in the distillery's portfolio.

Twenty-five years later, in early 2019, Kentucky Spirit's iconic "turkey feather" glass was changed to a much simpler and less ornate bottle style. While not as well received by everyone (including yours truly), I'll openly admit that this year's Kentucky Spirit remains signature Jimmy Russell at a consistently high quality. You might even say the profile bar has been raised a bit. At least, that's my experience as of late.

Regardless of bottle styles and labels, the most important thing is always the whiskey. At a time when American enthusiasts pay premiums for export eight-year age-stated Wild Turkey 101, they're either quick to forget or slow to remember that Wild Turkey Kentucky Spirit is essentially the very same thing in single-barrel representation. Factor in private selections and the odds are in your favor that you'll find a unique pour.

And that's the beauty of Kentucky Spirit. It's as if Jimmy Russell himself rolled out a special hand-selected barrel just for you: his timeless 101-proof Kentucky Straight bourbon whiskey. That's what Kentucky Spirit means to me. Sure, there's always Russell's Reserve Single Barrel Bourbon, but that's Eddie's baby. If you're looking for classic Jimmy Russell with a single-barrel spin, look no further than Wild Turkey Kentucky Spirit.

2. WILD TURKEY RARE BREED

Want to know a secret? Here goes . . . Wild Turkey Rare Breed is perhaps the most undervalued Kentucky straight bourbon whiskey on retail shelves today. I'll circle back to this shortly, but before I do, let's start from the beginning.

There are few people in the bourbon world that command attention like Jimmy Russell, but Jim Beam's Booker Noe was damn sure one of them. Honestly, if I could go back in time and interview one person in the industry, it would probably be Booker Noe. As diehard a Wild Turkey fan as I might be, I make no qualms about my semi-annual Booker's purchases. Unfortunately, its price has crept well above the everyman's budget. But fret not. We bourbon fans still have Jimmy Russell's affordable and widely available Rare Breed.

So, why this talk of Booker's when we should be talking about Rare Breed? Well, that's just it. There would probably be no Rare Breed were it not for

Booker's Bourbon. Introduced in 1988, Booker's cast the die for what consti-tutes a retail "small batch" bourbon, and it did so at full barrel strength (just how Booker Noe liked to sip it). Surprisingly (maybe unsurprisingly now), it caught on, and by 1991 it was time for Jimmy Russell to answer the call.

While the batches, bottles, and labels have changed multiple times over the past twenty-eight years, Wild Turkey Rare Breed has remained a consumer favorite. Some batches are better than others, but all stay true to Jimmy's original combination of pure barrel-proof six-, eight-, and twelve-year Kentucky straight bourbon whiskey. And just as it has from its intro-duction, Rare Breed still competes with Booker's—arguably more so now that Booker's is nearly double the price of Rare Breed.

Which brings me back to my initial assertion: Wild Turkey Rare Breed may be the most undervalued bourbon whiskey available today. For under $50 you're getting a six- to twelve-year, full-barrel-strength bourbon dis-tilled by the longest-tenured master distiller on Earth. No mysteries. No gimmicks. As Elmer T. Lee once remarked after nosing Rare Breed straight from the palms of his hands, "Pure Jimmy Russell."

Nailed it, Elmer.

1. WILD TURKEY 101

I'm sure it comes as no surprise that Wild Turkey 101 occupies the top spot on this list. It's the classic everyman's bourbon whiskey. Available, versatile, affordable, and undeniably delicious, there's very few bourbons—hell, very few whiskeys—that "check the boxes" like Wild Turkey 101. And what made that so? Jimmy Russell.

As many astute bourbon geeks know, Wild Turkey 101 originated in 1942, years before Jimmy Russell started working at Wild Turkey. (I'm betting young Jimmy was busy playing baseball and football with his school friends.) At that time Austin, Nichols' Wild Turkey 101 was a wholesaler's label, similar to something you'd find today at Costco. It was sourced from numerous distilleries in Kentucky, bottled and distributed nationwide. By 1971 Austin, Nichols zeroed in on a single quality source for their bourbon supply, J.T.S. Brown & Sons in Lawrenceburg, Kentucky, changing the name of the distillery and bourbon history forever. And the master distiller? You guessed it. Jimmy Russell.

Wild Turkey 101 may have originated in the mind of a Brooklyn executive, but the Wild Turkey 101 we know and enjoy today comes from the hard work and persistence of Jimmy Russell, *decades* of hard work and persistence. The recipe, yeast, and process are all Jimmy's classic, time-tested Anderson County magic. Even in modern times, with state-of-the-art facilities and computerized automation, 101 simply wouldn't taste like 101 without Jimmy's expertise and years of brand-defining influence.

If there's one bourbon whiskey that says, "Jimmy Russell," it's surely Wild Turkey 101. It belongs in every five-star establishment, every dive bar, every liquor cabinet, every suitcase, every flask, every cocktail or mixer, and every variation of whiskey glass known to man. It's as timeless as bourbon itself—the standard, the archetype, the mark of an American living legend.

I ask that you join me. Pour your favorite Wild Turkey and raise your glass to Jimmy Russell on his sixty-five years of remarkable, unparalleled service. Spread the word, share your bourbon, and above all else, savor every last drop and minute. Time is immeasurably valuable and never guaranteed. As such, live life to the fullest. Find your passion and stick with it. Live like Jimmy Russell, and you'll never work a day in your life. And if you're lucky, you might just do it for sixty-five years.

Cheers to Jimmy!

IF THERE'S ONE BOURBON WHISKEY
THAT SAYS, "JIMMY RUSSELL," IT'S SURELY
WILD TURKEY 101

An Open Letter to Jimmy Russell

An Open Letter To Jimmy Russell

The following letter was published on *Rare Bird 101* alongside "The Essence of Jimmy Russell."

SEPTEMBER 10, 2019

Dear Mr. Russell,

It is with pure gratitude and appreciation that I congratulate you on sixty-five years of service to the Wild Turkey Distillery and the bourbon industry. You are a champion of our nation's premier spirit, the keeper of the flame and living legacy of America's long and colorful distilling past. Your skill and dedication compose the roadmap to bourbon success (should individuals have your motivation and uncompromising attitude to follow it). Without you and your close-knit brotherhood of years past, bourbon may have been lost on the bottom shelf forever. Thankfully, your efforts ensured that never happened.

Hardly a day goes by that I fail to reflect on your invaluable contributions. While many seek the rarest, most luxurious bourbons on the market—paying astounding premiums unheard of decades ago—you've maintained products of consistent high quality and wide economic availability unparalleled in today's marketplace.

When I see the name "Jimmy Russell" on a label, I know exactly what I'm getting. I'm buying an honest-man's whiskey: a well-crafted spirit with a genuine Kentucky heritage. It's bold truth in an unpretentious, affordable bottle, and I thank you for that.

So, cheers to you on your sixty-fifth year, Mr. Russell! May your days be long and your glass always full of Wild Turkey.

Sincerely,

David Jennings

Rare Bird 101

The Best of 2019

To say 2019 was a busy year for me (and Wild Turkey) would be an understatement. I managed a Kickstarter publishing campaign, Wild Turkey released their first limited-edition rye whiskey, and Jimmy Russell celebrated his sixty-fifth anniversary at the distillery. What a year!

As for Wild Turkey's core bourbon and rye expressions, the quality had improved twofold. Deciding which whiskeys would make my annual Wild Turkey "best of" list was challenging. Thankfully, I had my Patreon supporters to lean on with the addition of a "Patron's Choice" award—a tradition that carried on to 2020 and beyond. dj

DECEMBER 17, 2019

Another year behind us. Another year to celebrate the best Wild Turkey has to offer. And what a year it's been! From exemplary core expressions to phenomenal single barrels, the options were far from limited. The Russells are at the top of their game. That's a fact. Please don't be fooled by those caught in the past. Yes, dusty pours are epic, but it's easy to forget that today's whiskeys are tomorrow's legends. And if there's a recent year to take note of, it's 2019.

CAMPARI WHISKEY BARONS BOND & LILLARD (BATCH 2)

Campari Whiskey Barons aren't strangers to these lists. Back in 2017, Bond & Lillard Batch 1, along with its co-release, Old Ripy, received my Best Design award. Outside of a new batch number, there were no apparent changes in Bond & Lillard's design for batch two. There was also no change in how stellar I think it looks. Countless bottles attempt to recreate or reimagine pre-Prohibition and medicinal whiskey styles, but very few achieve it with sheer classic elegance. Once again, bravissimo Campari design team!

BEST CORE EXPRESSION (2019)

RUSSELL'S RESERVE 10 YEAR OLD BOURBON

This may ruffle some Turkey feathers, but Russell's Reserve 10-Year has moved from one of my least favorite Wild Turkey expressions to one of my most frequently purchased. Why is that? I honestly don't know. But when I'm looking for an easy-sipping whiskey in the 90-proof range, I prefer it to showcase a nice oak presence regardless of ABV. Russell's Reserve 10-Year does that remarkably well. It also adds well-rounded character to cocktails and blends and doesn't cost a fortune.

There aren't many ten-year Kentucky straight bourbons priced in the $30 range (even fewer that can be found with ease) and only one that's brought to you by a team of master distillers with over 101 years of industry experience . . . Russell's Reserve 10 Year Old Bourbon.

BEST STRAIGHT BOURBON (2019)
WILD TURKEY 101

What can be said about Wild Turkey 101 that hasn't been said already? Those seeking a flavorful, well-crafted, and versatile bourbon without breaking the bank need only look for Wild Turkey 101. It's as simple as that.

This year's Wild Turkey 101 batches have been exceptional—not only living up to the surprisingly high bar set in 2018 but also exceeding it. What makes recent releases so impressive? Well, there's a lot of theories and rumors out there. What speaks loudest to me is the fact that the youngest bourbon in the 2018–2019 batches comes from the new distillery that opened in 2011. Not that Wild Turkey 101 incorporates youthful whiskey; to the contrary, I believe Master Distiller Eddie Russell has stated six to seven years as the current floor in terms of batch maturity. The ceiling, on the other hand, can cross the ten-year mark. All of this in a 101-proof bourbon that retails for a no-fuss $25 or less—a ridiculously delicious bourbon at that. Needless to say, 2019's Best Straight Bourbon is a no-brainer.

WILD TURKEY MASTER'S KEEP CORNERSTONE

Twenty-nineteen was a landmark year for Wild Turkey as it released its first limited-edition straight rye whiskey, Master's Keep Cornerstone. Boasting a selection of choice rye barrels ranging in age from nine to eleven years and bottled non-chill filtered at 109 proof, Cornerstone carried the specs that longtime Turkey rye lovers had been waiting for. And it delivered.

With notably complex layers of sweet and spicy texture, as well as a long, peppery finish that's uniquely "Camp Nelson," Master's Keep Cornerstone sets an impeccable tone for a new generation of Wild Turkey rye releases. Sure, its $175 price is a little hefty, and factoring that alongside the high quality of Russell's Reserve Single Barrel Rye, one could make a damn good argument for hesitation. Though, from my experience, judging a whiskey by its price is a slippery slope. The Russells aren't thinking about prices when they're producing whiskey; they're thinking about the quality of the whiskey itself. Bearing that in mind, I can only say this: if Master's Keep

Cornerstone is the foundation of Wild Turkey's revitalized rye program, we've got a hell of a lot to look forward to in the years ahead.

BEST SINGLE BARREL (2019)

SINGLE CASK NATION WILD TURKEY
(BARREL #17-759)

This was by far the award category I struggled with most. There were so many excellent single barrels this year: Wild Turkey Kentucky Spirit, Russell's Reserve Single Barrel, and of course, Single Cask Nation. And as badly as I wanted to place Moonshine Grill's "Cheesy Gold" in this spot, in a side-by-side tasting, Single Cask Nation's barrel #17-759 couldn't be beat—not even by a 12.5-year rarity. (Side note: if there were an honorable mention it would go to Moonshine Grill.)

What Joshua Hatton and Jason Johnstone-Yellin do for the whiskey community cannot be overstated. These guys are serious about whiskey, yet seriously fun all the same. They're also forth-right, generous, and have two of the most well-versed palates in the industry. When they commit to a barrel (or "cask" in the case of non-American spirits), they devote themselves to the essence of that spirit: its origin, brand, and nature of purpose. It's not about gimmicks or stickers. It's not about finding "the best." It's about finding barrels/casks that exemplify the range of a producer, from unmistakably "on profile" to undeniably unique.

Wild Turkey is no exception. This year's Single Cask Nation Wild Turkey releases are in many ways a juxtaposition of profiles. Barrel #18-428, which matured in Camp Nelson's rickhouse A, features intense, modern Wild Turkey notes with pepper-laden candy-esque sweetness. Barrel #17-759, which aged in Tyrone's rickhouse D, showcases classic Turkey attributes, loaded with buttery bakery notes and herbal/floral spice. A dream of a barrel to say the least and, therefore, my choice for 2019's Best Single Barrel.

It should be noted that bottling at barrel strength offers a slight advantage over Russell's Reserve Single Barrel, though it shouldn't discredit Joshua or Jason's talent. Everyone selects Wild Turkey barrels at barrel proof; it's the bottling proof that separates Single Cask Nation selections from Russell's Reserve. There's a certain satisfaction that comes with sipping undiluted single-barrel bourbon from your own glass, from your own bottle, at your own convenience (something Wild Turkey hasn't offered since the late 1990s). I propose that if Campari were to make that an option, the competition for this category would be overwhelming. And I'm totally fine with that. Campari, if you're reading this, let's make single-barrel, barrel-proof selections happen. Please.

Patrons' Choice (2019)
Campari Whiskey Barons W.B. Saffell
(Batch 1)

For those who are unaware, I have a Patreon website where I post regularly (almost every day). There's news, reviews, video livestreams, tastings, and occasional polls. My patrons play a critical role in what I do. They not only support my blog and related projects financially, they engage and communicate, not just with me but each other daily. They challenge and encourage me. It's a wonderful community, and I'm sincerely grateful and lucky to have it.

This year, I tried something new. Considering my patrons are some of the most dedicated Wild Turkey fans in the world, it only seemed appropriate for a "Patrons' Choice" award. Out of all of this year's releases (excluding private barrel selections), there was an indisputable favorite . . . Campari Whiskey Barons W.B. Saffell Batch 1.

I couldn't agree more. Crafted under the guidance of Master Distiller Eddie Russell, W.B. Saffell is a testament to his decades of blending experience. Composed of bourbon aged six, eight, ten, and twelve years, Saffell has much more to offer than many enthusiasts assume. It's not Rare Breed; it's not Wild Turkey 101. Saffell is a masterful batch of full-bodied bourbon with notable complexity and balance. I like to call it "2002 Junior," as it displays some of my favorite notes from the highly sought-after Russell's Reserve 2002.

Special thanks to my patrons for participating in this year's Patrons' Choice poll. You nailed it!

BEST WHISKEY OVERALL (2019)
WILD TURKEY RARE BREED
(BATCH 116.8)

If you had asked me about Wild Turkey Rare Breed several years ago, I would've told you you're better off finding another expression. In my opinion, Rare Breed Batch 112.8 was a significant step down in quality from its former batch, 03RB (2004-2013). Oh, how things have changed!

Not only has batch 116.8 turned the ship around, but it has done so with near-unanimous fanfare from whiskey critics and enthusiasts alike. Hell, it beat the entirety of the Buffalo Trace Antique Collection bourbon line in author Fred Minnick's Instagram blind-tasting livestream weeks ago. (I think some folks are still jaded about that one.)

But it doesn't take Fred Minnick, or me, or anyone else to show you how awesome Rare Breed is. One only needs to visit their favorite bar or bottle shop and try it for themselves. Unlike William Larue Weller or George T. Stagg, you'll actually find Rare Breed. And that's precisely what makes it 2019's "Best Overall." In this time of overpriced and excessively celebrated high-end whiskeys, Rare Breed remains a full-proof, zero-hype quality whiskey at an affordable price. It's Wild Turkey at its everyman's finest (Jimmy Russell's gift to the world) and, for many enthusiasts, the closest they'll get to sipping Wild Turkey straight from a barrel. Thank goodness we can all have that experience at our leisure.

What a great year to be a Turkey fan! So many reliable expressions, so many noteworthy single barrels. Could it get any better? Yes, I believe it can (and will). There are several things to look forward to already: Rare Breed Rye, Master's Keep Bottled in Bond, and an all-new range of rickhouses slated for the 2020 private barrel program. At this point, the sky's the limit, but for now, we'll enjoy the breadth of what we have, relish in its excellence, and raise a glass to Jimmy and Eddie for the fruits of their labor. Cheers!

WHAT A GREAT YEAR TO BE
A TURKEY FAN! ... RAISE A GLASS
TO JIMMY AND EDDIE FOR THE
FRUITS OF THEIR LABOR. CHEERS!

1974 WILD TURKEY 101 & FAREWELL TO AL YOUNG

*1974 Wild Turkey 101 &
Farewell to Al Young*

Al Young's passing hit harder than I could've imagined.
I never met the beloved Four Roses brand ambassador,
but his personal contributions to the bourbon community, not to mention a wealth of video interviews and
a book dedicated to the history of Four Roses Bourbon,
carry immeasurable worth to this day. This entry was
an effort to not only offer tribute and thanks to Mr.
Young but also to accentuate it with my appreciation for
bourbon history via a 1970's Wild Turkey 101. It's not
as lengthy or detailed as some of my other blog posts,
but it remains a personal favorite. Cheers to Al! dj

DECEMBER 31, 2019

Bourbon is rich with history. I mean that not only in the metaphorical
sense, but in the literal sense as well. With every pour you're experiencing history, the pride of the distiller, the craftsmanship of the cooper,
the life of the oak, the warmth of the summer sun, the chill of the winter
air, and the harmony that exists when mankind and Mother Nature work
together. There are seasons upon seasons in each glass . . . each bottle from
each batch, each batch from every single barrel. Some bourbons are older
than others, but no bourbon is without history.

This Christmas the bourbon community lost an icon. Al Young, Four Roses' incomparable senior brand ambassador and former plant manager passed away after more than fifty years of service in the bourbon industry. I never had the pleasure of meeting Mr. Young, though I'd wanted to for years. When I started writing my upcoming Wild Turkey book, *American Spirit*, it was Al Young's interviews for the University of Kentucky's Louie B. Nunn Center for Oral History that helped lay the groundwork. Not only did he interview Jimmy and Eddie Russell, but Thomas and Olivia Ripy, descendants of Lawrenceburg's famous whiskey baron, T.B. Ripy. I can't stress how important those interviews were to my research. I even found tremendous value in Mr. Young's own personal interviews, especially his recounting of meeting Jimmy Russell for the first time.

Al Young knew the value of a story. Stories are history and should be preserved for future generations (lest they be forgotten forever). Much of bourbon's history consists of tales passed down from generation to generation, distiller to distiller. Only in the past few decades have writers actually put these tales to paper in earnest, including Mr. Young, who authored *Four Roses: The Return of a Whiskey Legend*. It's my sincere hope that everyone who appreciates bourbon—from the casual sipper to the diehard enthusiast—realizes the significance of endeavors like Al Young's. The history of bourbon is an important thread in the fabric of our nation. The stories that define it deserve to be shared, and Mr. Young understood that. His contributions to our beloved hobby—to its very heritage—will surely be missed.

Speaking of history and sharing, today's pour wouldn't be possible without the help of a good friend and fellow Wild Turkey history buff, David James. David has been a Wild Turkey fan for decades and maintains a collection of genuinely rare Turkey artifacts that are impressive to say the least. In fact, he's in the process of constructing a Wild Turkey museum in his home state of New York. You can bet I'll be there when it opens!

Thanks to David, the bourbon I have the pleasure of reviewing today is a 1974 1/10-pint Wild Turkey 101 8-Year (in bottling line mint condition,

I might add). The fill level is perfect, the label is flawless, and the tax strip free from discoloration or damage of any kind. It's as if someone went back in time, purchased this bottle, returned, and placed it in my hands. Interestingly, it was likely sitting on a retail shelf when Al Young first met Jimmy Russell in 1976. Every bourbon tells a story, and I'm guessing this one's just getting started.

Wild Turkey 101 (1974)

SPIRIT:	Kentucky straight bourbon whiskey
PROOF:	101
AGE:	eight years
MISC.:	bottled by the Austin, Nichols Distilling Co., Lawrenceburg, KY
	tasted neat in a Glencairn Glass after a few minutes rest…
COLOR:	deep copper
NOSE:	(intense dusty Wild Turkey) honey-maple, blood orange, brandied
	cherries, funky oak, stovetop vanilla pudding, caramel, herbal
	spice, floral perfume, tobacco, leather, nutmeg, faint mineral notes
TASTE:	(oily mouthfeel) vanilla syrup, dense honey-maple, caramel, orange
	peel, fruit cocktail, sweet musty oak, brown sugar, herbal tea,
	nutmeg, hints of tobacco
FINISH:	long, warm and flavorful—rich vanilla, toasted caramel, charred
	oak, herbal and floral spice, cinnamon, clove tobacco, sweet/zesty
	pepper, orange liqueur, traces of minerality

OVERALL:

Yet another fine example of the beauty of vintage Wild Turkey bourbon. There's intensity and density in its notes, but it neither overwhelms nor confounds the senses. This is in many ways the essence of American whiskey from decades past: unique complexity achieved without the need for a high bottling proof (primarily due to a low barrel-entry proof). Add to that the absence of chill filtration and various contributing factors (like notably older whiskey in common everyday batches) and you end up with a product that's impractical and/or preventatively costly to recreate today.

INTENSE DUSTY

TURKEY

As for this particular 1974 Wild Turkey 101 8-Year, it's not the best dusty I've ever had, but it's no slouch of a pour either. All of the typical dusty Turkey notes are found here in one phase or another (nose, taste, finish). There's also a slight minerality that I've picked up before in older bottles of Wild Turkey 101 (1979 and 1989 immediately come to mind). I wouldn't go so far as to call it George Dickel's signature "Flintstone vitamin" note, but it borders on it. Maybe "Dickel-esque" in some ways? Regardless, it's there and, frankly, I like it. It gives this pour character and balances out some of the sweeter notes. In fact, this may be the most balanced dusty Turkey I've ever tasted. Truly an exquisite bourbon, and I wish it could never end.

It's whiskey like this that spurs reflection on bourbon's past in a profound, personal way. Our country's history can easily be experienced through our senses. One only needs to visit a museum, battlefield, national monument, or talk with one's elders. There you can see and hear history. But consider this: with bourbon, you can smell and taste history. More importantly, you don't need a rare or vintage bottle to grant you that experience. Any bourbon enjoyed in the right mindset or company will get you there.

And with that, I encourage you to take a few extra moments with your next pour. Briefly research what you're drinking. Maybe find a video (perhaps one of Al Young's) and learn the story behind your whiskey. I believe you'll find a greater appreciation for what you're sipping, and I'd like to think Mr. Young would have agreed.

Top 10 Sentimental Turkeys

Whiskey top-ten lists are a dime a dozen. When I first started my blog, I was eager to create an evolving list of the ten best Turkeys. As I grew in the hobby, tasting more and more expressions (especially Wild Turkey), I realized maintaining such a list was daunting. In fact, I still struggle with my blog's top ten. How can one accurately rank one exemplary whiskey over another, particularly when the palate is affected by circumstances and mood? I'm not saying it's completely impossible, but it damn near is.

There are, however, favorites I'll never forget—whiskeys that mean something greater than exclusivity or extraordinary taste. They're my sentimental pours. Everyone has their favorites; these are mine as of spring 2020. dj

MAY 12, 2020

You see a lot of "top ten" whiskey lists nowadays. They're often found in mainstream online publications, typically providing little substance or relative value to knowledgeable enthusiasts. I've attempted my own top ten, though it's admittedly far from perfect. In fact, I received a question from a reader this week asking for clarification as to why specific expressions I've rated highly weren't noted. And that's when it dawned on me: emotion plays a major role in my selection and ranking process.

All things considered, it's past time that I revisit my top ten—redevelop and restructure it, even. But before I do, I thought it might be fun to devise a list that's beyond profile or price. It's a list of Wild Turkey expressions that mean a lot to me personally. Some are rare, some are vintage, but overall, they're each memorable in their own way.

I proudly present my *Top 10 Sentimental Favorite Wild Turkey Expressions*.

10. Wild Turkey Master's Keep Decades (2017)

If you're looking for an ideal example of a well-crafted, mature straight bourbon blend, look no further than Master's Keep Decades. Consisting of barrels aged ten to twenty years, Decades is a tribute to both Eddie Russell's thirty-fifth year of service and a testament to the legacy of his father, Jimmy. But as fantastic as it may taste, its profile has the uncanny ability to transport me back to my childhood.

When I was a youngster, my dad often carried a roll of Certs candies in his blazer pocket. He didn't part with them easily, but if my brothers and I got to wiggling at church, well, out came the Certs! I find the memory of Certs, specifically orange Certs, when nosing and tasting Master's Keep Decades. It never fails. Any whiskey that sends you back in time is worthy of a spot on one's all-time sentimental favorites.

THERE ARE, HOWEVER, FAVORITES I'LL NEVER FORGET - WHISKEYS THAT MEAN SOMETHING GREATER THAN EXCLUSIVITY OR EXTRAORDINARY TASTE.

9. Russell's Reserve Single Barrel Bourbon: Farris & Dedman, #68-G-4

In 2018, I was fortunate to acquire a Russell's Reserve Single Barrel Bourbon selected by Jamie Farris of Lincoln Road Package Store and Dixon Dedman of Kentucky Owl. While the whiskey was excellent in virtually every way, it was the conversations I had with both Jamie and Dixon that made the experience special. The men are complimentary about each other's palate, and both are nothing if not humble when it comes to what they do. As such, I was moved to post Dixon's email on my blog detailing the story of how this Russell's Reserve bottle came to be. The bourbon itself didn't last long. And if there's one barrel I could go back in time and taste again, Farris & Dedman #68-G-4 would surely place high on that list.

8. Russell's Reserve Single Barrel Bourbon: Lincoln Road #1-A-4

Speaking of Jamie Farris, he's gracing this list again. In the fall of 2017, I lucked upon Jamie's first Russell's Reserve Single Barrel private selection. Not only was it the older "tear/craft strip" label, but it was signed by then Associate Master Distiller Eddie Russell. Sure, Wild Turkey bottles signed by Eddie aren't exactly uncommon today, but it added a layer of uniqueness to an already unique bourbon. On a phone call, Jamie patiently talked to me about its origin and the conversation stretched into all kinds of . . . well, "cool bourbon talk."

Subject: No Subject
Date: Monday, April 2, 2018 at 11:05:24 AM Eastern Daylight Time
From: Dixon Dedman
To: rarebird101@protonmail.com

The story of barrel sixty-eight is hazy at best. It was just Eddie, Jamie, and me that day, and we'd already picked barrels at Four Roses that morning. There's a certain familiarity you develop with Eddie when he becomes comfortable with you and you're not dragging along ten other people—taking pics for Instagram and posting all over social media. Eddie always has something to share with us and we usually bring Eddie something as well. Honestly, I think Eddie gets tired of everyone always asking questions about why they don't make Turkey that tastes like old Turkey and things like that. I think because we're there to select barrels and have a great relationship with him (Jamie even more so than me), he gets really excited about just drinking amazing barrels with some easy-going guys who aren't going to pester him with all kinds of goofy questions.

At any rate, I respect those that compile laundry lists of tasting notes and are very introspective about the process. We, however, do not. It's a glass and a bottle of water—that's about it. We don't ask about the rickhouse or the age. We don't really care about any of the specifics or that type of thing. We go by what comes out of the barrel.

The long and short of it is that we tasted barrel sixty-eight on a previous pick. I don't recall what we selected in its place, but Jamie probably does because he has that type of memory. We tasted through probably a dozen barrels, and while we found some we liked, we weren't thrilled. Eddie said we could go over to the other side of the rickhouse and look at some of those barrels. Seriously, Jamie has an encyclopedic memory for this stuff, and when we walked past the barrels, he said, "Isn't that the low-yield barrel that was here last time?" Sure enough, it was. We pulled a sample, tasted it, and said, "Why the hell is this still here?" Eddie was equally perplexed. He liked it as much as we did. Nothing else that day came close. So, the barrel we passed on once was still there when we went back, and we opted not to pass on it a second time.

When the barrel came in, Jamie called me. He said, "Dude, no joke. That barrel sixty-eight is the best barrel we've ever picked from Turkey hands down." I honestly thought he was full of shit. So, he brought me some bottles from some other picks and a few from sixty-eight. I called him back after I opened them to confirm that he was right. It's the best barrel we've ever picked from Turkey.

So, that's what I remember from the pick of barrel sixty-eight. It's pretty cool to have the opportunity to help Jamie with some of these picks. He has an incredible talent for recognizing good barrels, and he's no-nonsense about it. I think that's why his barrel program is so successful. Not to mention, when you've got Eddie weighing in as opposed to just administering the pick, you end up with something even more special.

It should also be noted that while his name is not listed on the neck tag for barrel eight-four, Jamie was very much a part of that pick, and helped select that barrel as well. So, this is actually a Farris/Dedman v. Dedman/Farris slugfest. May the best team win.

Dixon Dedman

PHOTO BY
DAVID JENNINGS

There's one thing I'll say about Jamie Farris: he knows bourbon. He knows it from experience by getting out there and tasting it in rickhouses, barrel after barrel (after barrel). And it can't be understated: he's remarkably humble and never pretends to be anything other than himself. Not only am I a fan of Jamie's devotion, talent, and humility, I know that Eddie Russell is as well.

7. 1992 "CHEESY GOLD FOIL" WILD TURKEY 101 12-YEAR

Ah, the revered Wild Turkey "Cheesy Gold Foil" (or "CGF" for short). To many, it's the ultimate Wild Turkey expression. For me, it all depends on the year/batch. While 1992 isn't a personal favorite profile-wise, it earns a place on this top ten by being the first Wild Turkey 12-Year I ever tasted (my second ever dusty Turkey pour). I owe this special experience to the generosity of an extraordinary bourbon friend, who I'll discuss in greater detail shortly. For now, know that your first time tasting Wild Turkey 101/12 will likely be memorable. Those who've already had the pleasure can certainly attest.

6. SINGLE CASK NATION: WILD TURKEY BARREL #16-313

This monster single barrel from the sixth floor of Tyrone's rickhouse K deserves a place on this list for several reasons. I could go on indefinitely about its stellar "best-of-the-best" profile (and have before), but above all else stands the thoughtfulness of Joshua Hatton and Jason Johnstone-Yellin.

In 2019, I held my first annual Patreon gathering in Lexington, Kentucky. Wild Turkey fans from all around brought their most cherished pours. In a lineup that included CGF, "Split Label" 101/12, Rare Breed batch 01-99, various rarities and sought-after limited editions, Single Cask Nation #16-313 held its own in glorious fashion. What struck me as equally impressive was the fact that despite not being able to attend the gathering, Jason donated this bottle from his personal collection for all to enjoy. And enjoy it we did! Each time this Single Cask Nation selection comes to mind, it's accompanied by memories of last year's gathering. And I think that says it all right there.

5. 1994 WILD TURKEY KENTUCKY SPIRIT "PEWTER TOP"

Back in my diehard days of Reddit's r/Bourbon and r/Scotchswap, I had the pleasure of meeting some truly passionate whiskey fans, many of whom I've gotten to know and talk with outside of those forums. One such redditor is u/MikeCzyz.

Even then, Wild Turkey Kentucky Spirit was about what it is today: a tenured, single-barrel bourbon expression standing in the shadow of Russell's Reserve Single Barrel Bourbon. Be that as it may, it maintained its army of unwavering champions. Mike was (and remains) one of the few and the proud. And when it comes to Kentucky Spirit, no two words carry more weight than "pewter top." Thankfully, Mike was willing to share his 1994 inaugural bottle of Wild Turkey Kentucky Spirit in 2017 and, damn, was it delicious. To date, it's the best Kentucky Spirit I've ever tasted, and I hope to one day enjoy another mid-1990s release.

4. 2016 Whisky Jewbilee: Wild Turkey Barrel #2931

In 2017, I received a message on Reddit from author and spirits writer Aaron Goldfarb. After a few exchanges, he published "How Wild Turkey Funk Became a Whiskey Geek Obsession" for *PUNCH* magazine. Seemingly overnight, this blog received significant traffic, at least more than I'd ever witnessed at the time. It was then I realized that Wild Turkey had the potential to reach a wider audience; it just needed a louder voice. I set out on a mission to try to make that happen. It wasn't so much for me as it was for others. If I could find happiness in a brand that's affordable and easily found, thousands of whiskey enthusiasts might do the same.

Shortly after the article, Aaron introduced me to J&J Spirits, sharing the last of his treasured 2016 Whisky Jewbilee from Wild Turkey's rickhouse O. I was mesmerized. Single-barrel Wild Turkey bottled at full barrel proof (non-chill filtered, no less) . . . wowzah! Why wasn't Campari doing this? Thank goodness J&J was able to crack that code (albeit not near enough as I'd like) and shine a brief light on the magnificence of straight-from-a-barrel Turkey.

I should also mention that Aaron's gesture led me to Joshua Hatton, who kindly set aside time for my first official blog interview. Ever since, both Joshua and Jason have been friends, supporters, and jovial advocates of Wild Turkey and my blog. There's a number of wonderful personalities in the whiskey community. As far as I'm concerned, Joshua and Jason are two of the finest. Oh, and Aaron's not so bad himself.

3. Russell's Reserve Single Barrel Bourbon: "Promise to Mr. PorkChop"

In one's lifetime, there are a handful of days that are never forgotten. Some are joyful, some are tragic. And, every once in a while, an opportunity emerges to reconcile the past—perhaps not entirely, but enough to find peace or meaning in the madness. Such was the case when I had the privilege of helping select a Russell's Reserve Single Barrel Bourbon in memory of Roy "Mr. PorkChop" Alves.

It was my first Wild Turkey barrel selection at the distillery. Standing in Tyrone's rickhouse A, with its 125-year history going back to James Porter Ripy and Old Hickory Springs in 1894, you could smell decades upon decades of innumerable barrels that once granted their essence to the angels. On that first floor, our group chose the most fitting barrel for Mr. PorkChop, a 122-proof bruiser of unforgettable flavor.

Looking back, the day seemed like a dream, and I think of it often. A group of friends on the trip of a lifetime, sipping Kentucky's finest with Eddie Russell. And at the heart of our assembly, a barrel to serve as a tribute to a father sorely missed. Bourbon can't heal wounds, but in the right company it can warm the heart and touch the soul.

Cheers to Mr. PorkChop!

2. 1974 WILD TURKEY 101

As big a Wild Turkey fan as I may be, I stand on the shoulders of giants. One of those giants is Mr. David James. David has amassed a collection of Wild Turkey artifacts and curiosities worthy of a two-part *American Pickers* episode. (Hmm . . . may need to make that happen.)

Last New Year's Eve, I opened one of those artifacts: a 1974 Wild Turkey 101 1/10 pint (thank you again, David). While not Four Roses, it was (to me) the perfect whiskey to celebrate the life of the incomparable Al Young. How so? Without Al's passion for bourbon history, I might still be writing my upcoming Wild Turkey book. His interviews with Jimmy and Eddie Russell, as well as Tom and Olivia Ripy, were in many ways the genesis of my first manuscript. Al's work was immeasurable, as was the happiness imparted by the amazing '74 101, and I'm eternally grateful to both Al and David for all they've done for me.

1. 1981 WILD TURKEY 101

Everyone has their first dusty Wild Turkey. For me it was a 1981 Wild Turkey 101, and it proved the catalyst of this incredible journey I currently travel. The grand majority of us don't stumble upon dusty Wild Turkey by chance. It's shared with us through friends and timely acquaintances. Which is exactly what happened back in 2016, when a kind Redditor realized my appreciation for everyday Wild Turkey was only the beginning.

I'm unsure of exactly what motivated this generous internet stranger. One might call it fate, but to do so draws attention away from the act of kindness itself. I choose to believe he saw what many of us see in each other. We see the magic of discovery and realize that there's more to bourbon than highly allocated releases or repetitive sought-after labels. It resonates with all of us—the pure desire to share, celebrate, collaborate, and discuss. It's the crux of our hobby. Without it, we're merely "drinkers" or "collectors."

So, thank you, Chris Toner, for that opportunity years ago. Sure, it's possible I would've discovered vintage Wild Turkey at some point (my love for modern 101 was strong enough at the time to warrant it), yet one never knows. I don't question the past. I accept it. I try my best to embrace it. And unless some tragedy befalls me or my beloved spirit of choice, I'll forever be an evangelist for Wild Turkey. I sincerely hope that, one day, you'll all be too.

MY TOP 10 SENTIMENTAL WHISKEYS

1.

2.

3.

4.

5.

6.

7.

8.

9.

10.

WILD TURKEY SINGLE BARREL PRIMER

Wild Turkey Single Barrel Primer

Interest in single-barrel whiskey expressions has grown significantly in the last five years. Shortly after participating in the 2020 Whiskey from Home event (an online festival following the onset of the COVID-19 pandemic), I received a number of emails and social media messages regarding Wild Turkey private barrels and single-barrel expressions. It seemed only appropriate to author a post describing each available offering, as well as sharing my recommendations aimed at one's personal profile preferences. dj

JULY 28, 2020

What do you consider the criteria for an exemplary barrel of whiskey? Complexity? Maturity? Balance? Uniqueness? Rarity? Or perhaps it's something harder to nail down—a sipping experience that confounds or stirs emotion.

Ultimately, one must decide what they're looking for as a whiskey enthusiast. If rarity is an important aspect of a single-barrel whiskey, then the rest of this post likely won't appeal to you. That being said, single-barrel releases are inherently uncommon in terms of bottle count. Take Russell's Reserve Single Barrel private selections, for example. I've seen bottle counts as low as forty-two and as high as 180. One might call that rare—incredibly rare when focusing on a particular low-yield barrel. But then, with 600–800 (or more) barrels in the distillery's barrel program year after year, and given vast subjectivity when it comes to the interpretation of profile variance, rarity starts looking more and more . . . common. And let's not forget, thousands of barrels are aging gracefully at Wild Turkey as I type.

So, we're left with quality, as defined by transparency, flavor profile, and the overall sipping experience. We're talking about the whiskey itself, not the fancy bottle, box, label, tag, sticker, wax, felt bag, "gotta catch 'em all" alpha/letter, or hokey story about grandpa's recipe or colonial generals.

Who made the whiskey? How did they make it? How does it taste? How does it make you feel?

The answers to these questions are key.

Bold. Genuine. True.

There are numerous distilleries in Kentucky alone, even more when you include Indiana, Tennessee, and others. I can't speak for all of them, but I can say that when it comes to Wild Turkey, one can easily discover barrels of the highest quality with memorable profiles. Complexity, maturity, balance, uniqueness are all found with minimal effort. And perhaps most importantly, they're brought to you by the longest-tenured distilling team in the world. There's no mystique, tall tales, or smoke and mirrors. Distilled, barreled, aged, bottled, and approved by the Russells . . . that's it.

Whether you're considering an everyday bottle of Wild Turkey Kentucky Spirit or Russell's Reserve Single Barrel, take comfort that what you're purchasing is reflective of Jimmy and Eddie Russell's dedication to craft. As for private selection bottles, know that the Russells (primarily Eddie) oversee each barrel in the program. That isn't to say that Eddie gives vendors a short leash. To the contrary: he wants individuals and groups to find barrels that speak to them. He appreciates profile variance and the thrill of the hunt just as much as a seasoned enthusiast (arguably more). Hell, it's his job.

Considering this post is a primer, I'll cut to the chase and touch on each of Wild Turkey's current single-barrel offerings. (I won't be covering vintage single-barrel releases like Kentucky Legend or Heritage.) Veteran bourbon fans, particularly ones who've read my book, *American Spirit*, might find some of this information repetitive. But hey, stick around. You never know what's around the corner!

WILD TURKEY KENTUCKY SPIRIT

Though not as popular as it has been in years past, Kentucky Spirit was Wild Turkey's first single-barrel expression. Introduced in 1994 and bottled at the brand's signature 101 proof, Kentucky Spirit began as a means for Master Distiller Jimmy Russell to showcase his finest barrels at a familiar ABV. Through the years the bottle design has changed, as has the bourbon contained within, though it remains an important representation of Jimmy's cherished spirit.

WILD TURKEY KENTUCKY SPIRIT

AGE: No age stated (reportedly eight to ten years)

PROOF: 101

CHILL FILTRATION: Yes

PRICE: About $65

GENERAL PROFILE TASTING NOTES (BARREL DEPENDENT): vanilla, toffee, sweet oak, baked goods, hints of citrus and herbal/floral spice

RECOMMENDATION: Those who favor Wild Turkey 101 are sure to find common ground with Wild Turkey Kentucky

Spirit. But then, that may be Kentucky Spirit's greatest weakness. With a notable price disparity between the two expressions, it warrants a truly special barrel to justify Kentucky Spirit's overall expense. For me, it's well worth a gamble. And while I can't say that every Kentucky Spirit has impressed me, when an exemplary bottle is found, it's quite the irreplaceable treasure.

If you're looking for a Wild Turkey barrel rooted in the 101 profile, though typically more refined and finessed, Kentucky Spirit is your first stop.

Russell's Reserve Single Barrel Bourbon

In 2013, then Associate Master Distiller Eddie Russell found himself cultivating a new single-barrel expression. Of course, it had to meet Jimmy Russell's approval, but I'm willing to bet that wasn't too difficult a task. After all, we're talking about one of the most impressive expressions ever released by Wild Turkey: Russell's Reserve Single Barrel Bourbon. To this day Russell's Reserve Single Barrel remains a favorite among diehard bourbon enthusiasts. For the price, its high-quality variance and consistent excellence isn't easily matched.

RUSSELL'S RESERVE SINGLE BARREL BOURBON

AGE: No age stated* (reportedly eight to ten years)

PROOF: 110

CHILL FILTRATION: No

PRICE: About $60

GENERAL PROFILE TASTING NOTES (BARREL DEPENDENT): caramel, toasted vanilla, brown sugar, honey-maple, charred oak, rich baking spice, dark fruit, leather

*Private selection bottlings state the date distilled, dumped, and bottled as of mid-2019.

RECOMMENDATION: Those seeking a full-flavored, more "true to the barrel" sipping experience should find a lifelong companion with Russell's Reserve Single Barrel Bourbon. While not full-barrel proof (What's up with that, Campari?), it's bottled only five points away from barrel-entry proof (from 115 to 110). It's also non-chill filtered. I'll spare you the science of chill filtration (Google is your friend), but essentially, it's a cosmetic process that producers employ to beautify whiskey. The downside is a thinner mouthfeel, and many argue thinner flavor as well. Fortunately, with Russell's Reserve Single Barrel, you don't have to worry about that.

Russell's Reserve Single Barrel Rye

Building on the success of 2013's Russell's Reserve Single Barrel Bourbon, and Eddie Russell's new fascination with rye whiskey (thanks largely to his son Bruce Russell), 2015 welcomed another rye expression to the lineup: Russell's Reserve Single Barrel Rye. Whereas Wild Turkey 101 Rye became a bartender's secret weapon, and Russell's Reserve 6-Year Rye an everyman's balanced easy sipper, Russell's Reserve Single Barrel Rye targets the savvy rye whiskey consumer looking for a unique experience from each fresh cork pop.

RUSSELL'S RESERVE SINGLE BARREL RYE

AGE: No age stated (reportedly six to eight years)

PROOF: 104

CHILL FILTRATION: No

PRICE: About $70

GENERAL PROFILE TASTING NOTES (BARREL DEPENDENT): vanilla frosting, caramel drizzle, honey, sweet charred oak, lemon peel, light baking spice and floral notes

RECOMMENDATION: Enthusiasts who appreciate a flavorful and complex rye whiskey with plenty of Kentucky character should give Russell's Reserve Single Barrel Rye a whirl. At roughly $70, it punches above its price in consideration of several popular rye whiskeys of similar age and proof. Personally, I find it stands its ground remarkably well against popular limited editions, like Thomas H. Handy and Kentucky Owl Rye (and easier to find too). In fact, Russell's Reserve Single Barrel

Rye is my favorite Wild Turkey rye expression, and that includes Master's Keep Cornerstone and Rare Breed Rye.

As for Russell's Reserve Single Barrel Rye private selections, you probably won't find them anytime soon (the latest I've seen is 2017). First, Wild Turkey rye stocks number considerably less than bourbon stocks. And while production has ramped up over the years, there's still a way to go. Second, there's been no TTB COLA registration for a Russell's Reserve Single Barrel Rye private selection label similar to the bourbon label approved in 2019. Until we see a label filing, I doubt you'll find new rye private selections sporting the old neck tag and retail label combo (though one never knows). But don't let that get you down. Consider this: the same barrels a group would select from are likely (almost surely) the very same barrels Eddie earmarks for retail Russell's Reserve Single Barrel bottlings. No stickers. No hype. No FOMO.

Wrapping Up

There's a sea of single-barrel whiskeys out there to choose from. Few, however, are backed by a level of expertise and legacy comparable to the Russells'. That doesn't mean other distilleries can't produce exemplary barrels of whiskey (be it bourbon or rye). They damn well do. There's just something satisfying about a quality single-barrel expression that's relatively easy to find and afford. Each barrel carries with it a chance, a roll of the dice. Sometimes you win. Sometimes you win big. But in House Russell, there's seldom any losers.

WILD TURKEY CYPB (CRAFT YOUR PERFECT BIRD)

Wild Turkey CYPB (Craft Your Perfect Bird)

In 2015, Buffalo Trace Distillery announced its "Craft Your Perfect Bourbon" (CYPB) project. Consumers could design their ideal bourbon through a series of questions online. Based on the results of the survey, the first Weller CYPB was released in 2018. It continues to this day as a popular (and difficult to acquire) crowd-sourced expression.

The success of Buffalo Trace's initiative, combined with whiskey enthusiasts' affection for age-stated Wild Turkey 101, started me thinking . . . *What if I could craft my own perfect Turkey?* With so many expressions in Wild Turkey's portfolio, it had to be possible. As it turned out, it was easier than I expected and fun, too! dj

SEPTEMBER 8, 2020

You've heard it countless times: "Bring back eight-year 101!" I get it. I'd love to see an eight-year age statement on Wild Turkey 101. Hell, we all would. But if you think about it, eight-year, 101-proof Wild Turkey already exists (and I don't mean the Japanese export). It's called Kentucky Spirit. There's also Russell's Reserve Single Barrel Bourbon, which is 110 proof and typically aged eight to ten years. Each of those are excellent alternatives. Besides, adding an age statement to domestic Wild Turkey 101 would only increase the price of an already phenomenal value bourbon. And no one wants that.

But what if I told you there's a way to craft your own eight-year Wild Turkey 101? No, it doesn't require a collection of rare or vintage components. It doesn't even require limited editions or sought-after private selections. Not at all. You only need two ingredients, both of which can be found at your friendly neighborhood liquor store: Russell's Reserve 10-Year and Russell's Reserve Single Barrel Bourbon.

Blending Wild Turkey expressions isn't an uncommon subject. I've covered more than a few in the past several years. Some, like "W.B. Hackell," I enjoy on a regular basis (enough to fashion a handle worth this summer). I even crafted a 101-esque blend back in 2018 to mimic classic Wild Turkey. Unfortunately, it requires Master's Keep 17-Year, which isn't so easy to find nowadays. But that hasn't stopped me from revisiting the "improved 101" concept. What it comes down to is simple science with a creative kicker—an equal-parts, fixed-proof blend with infinite flavor profile potential.

Let's start with the first component, Russell's Reserve 10-Year. This readily available 90-proof bourbon can be found for $30 to $40 almost anywhere fine liquors are sold. Though sub-101 proof, it maintains a maturity uncommonly found in bourbons its price (Eagle Rare is one that comes to mind). It's also flavorful, consistent, and easy to appreciate, be it neat, on the rocks, or in a cocktail (I hanker a Boulevardier myself). It won't blow you away with layered complexity or boldness, but that's not what Eddie Russell has in mind with this particular expression. Today's Russell's 10-Year is a well-batched, mid-shelf daily sipper. Nothing more, nothing less.

I recently discovered my first 2020 bottling of Russell's Reserve 10-Year on a casual shopping trip (one of the perks of being a dedicated Turkey fan is finding joy in everyday bottles). This particular batch was bottled on February 3 (for more information on Wild Turkey bottle codes, please refer to my online guide at RareBird101.com). I'll spare a full review (it's unquestionably as good or better than the 2018–2019 batches I've had), but here's some general tasting notes for reference: *toasted caramel, cherry pie, fragrant charred oak, licorice, clove, vanilla bean; medium finish with leather, dark citrus, diminishing herbal spice.*

Damn . . . this bourbon only gets better each year! Eddie Russell once mentioned thirteen-year whiskey finding its way into Russell's Reserve 10-Year. It wouldn't surprise me if this 2020 batch has thirteen-, fifteen-, or even seventeen-year whiskey in it. Pure speculation, of course. But I wouldn't doubt it for one second. The oak influence is unmistakable—arguably magical.

Moving along to the heftier half of this 101/8 blend, Russell's Reserve Single Barrel Bourbon. You can opt for the standard retail iteration or a private barrel selection. The choice is yours. That being said, I think you'll find a greater appreciation when experimenting with different bottles of

Russell's Reserve Single Barrel. Blending with private selections helps tremendously, as you have rickhouse and floor information, as well as maturity (distilled, dumped, and bottling dates) thanks to the mid-2019 label update.

For today's illustration, I'm using a Russell's Reserve private selection (#20-1171) from Lincoln Road Package Store in Hattiesburg, MS. Aged eight years on the fourth floor of Tyrone B (the second oldest rickhouse at Wild Turkey), it features a balanced, confectionary-centered profile. My tasting notes are as follows: *vanilla, honey-butter, caramel drizzle, sweet oak, maple candy, warm baking spice; medium-long finish with toffee, brown sugar glaze, faint orange peel and clove.*

As expected, a rock-solid Russell's pick, one that should complement the leather and earthier oak tones of 2020's Russell's 10-Year. With that, let's blend!

This is where the fun begins. And the best part? There's no measuring cups, droppers, or hydrometers needed. Simply add equal parts of each whiskey in a glass and you'll end up at 100 proof every time. Introduce a pinch more Russell's Reserve Single Barrel to bump the proof to 101. (If you want precision, a 45/55 blend of Russell's 10-Year and Russell's Reserve Single Barrel will equal 101 proof exactly.) Give it a swirl, a few minutes of rest, then dive right in.

Upon nosing, you'll immediately notice your creation showcases both similarities and differences with its originating parts. You're likely to discover new profile notes as well. Here's what I'm getting from today's example: *vanilla bean, salted caramel, dense oak, nutmeg, baked cinnamon and brown sugar, hints of honey maple; medium-long finish with molasses, herbal tea, cola, diminishing leather and pepper.*

While this combination isn't miles apart from Wild Turkey 101, it's complex and finessed—and, as such, a notable improvement. And it should be. After all, both Russell's Reserve 10-Year and Russell's Reserve Single Barrel Bourbon are super-premium expressions. But this is only one example. Depending on which Russell's Reserve Single Barrel bottle you select for your blend, you're sure to end up with something altogether different—potentially stunning, even. It's all up to you!

And if you do end up with something out of this world (a truly amazing FrankenTurkey) what next? Own it! Fill an empty Wild Turkey 101 bottle (of any size) and personalize it with a sticker or your own handcrafted art. I'm not saying to market it, sell it, or any of that ridiculous (illegal) funny business; to the contrary, this exercise is for your own satisfaction and joy (and the occasional share or brag among your bourbon friends).

So, what are you waiting for? Get up and start crafting your own 101/8! Worst-case scenario, you end up with excellent whiskey and a damn good time. I'd call that a win.

WHISKEY
TIME CAPSULE

Whiskey Time Capsule

Each fall sees the release of highly sought-after annual limited-edition bourbons: Pappy Van Winkle, Buffalo Trace Antique Collection, Old Forester Birthday Bourbon, etc. Each time, the whiskey world goes nuts. What we often fail to realize is the best bourbons are already sitting on the shelves of your local liquor store.

Take, for example, today's vintage bottle marketplace, particularly for Wild Turkey. Prices have climbed dramatically, yet these bottles were at one time standard offerings priced for the everyday consumer. Sure, they taste fantastic and present a flavor profile seldom (if ever) found in modern whiskey; however, one might very well say the same thing about today's whiskey forty years from now.

This piece was written to steer enthusiasts away from the irritation and expense of chasing contemporary rarities. Those who take these words to heart might just end up with an incredible dusty whiskey cabinet later in life. Worst-case scenario, they'll have a cabinet full of affordable, high-quality bourbon and rye whiskey. dj

September 22, 2020

I've got a thought exercise for you. Imagine every single whiskey you love has disappeared from shelves: no Wild Turkey 101, no Rare Breed, no Russell's Reserve Single Barrel. And let's not limit it to just Wild Turkey: no Evan Williams, no Eagle Rare, no Knob Creek. It's all gone, never to be seen again. Which bottles would you miss the most? Forget about rarity or valuation. Which whiskeys would you most miss sipping?

If you're honest with yourself, I think you'll find the majority of expressions making your list aren't necessarily difficult to find. They're probably not expensive either. They're the bourbon and rye whiskeys you appreciate more often than any others: your fundamentals, your "old reliables," your "dailys." Sometimes these expressions change, but we all have our long-standing mainstays.

THE IMPOSSIBLE COLLECTION

This past week the Bourbon Pursuit podcast featured writer Clay Risen. For those unaware, Clay authored *American Whiskey, Bourbon & Rye: A Guide to the Nation's Favorite Spirit* (as well as other acclaimed books). You can also find him on the Spirits Network and *Bourbon+* magazine. It's a fantastic episode, and I highly recommend checking it out if you're into whiskey, writing, or both. In the Bourbon Pursuit interview, the topic of bourbon hunting came up, and touched on how, looking back, Clay wished he'd purchased more of the whiskeys he cherished so much in the mid-2000s (many that are especially sought after today).

That discussion started me thinking. We live in a world of whiskey excess. There are high-quality bourbon and rye bottles seemingly everywhere. Hell, they're all around us. We've just tuned them out. They're like static: always there, never changing. No, I'm not talking about Pappy or BTAC or whatever wax-dipped "sticker-gamed" monstrosity everyone's clamoring over. I'm talking about your fundamentals, your "old reliables," your "dailys." The very stuff you and I take for granted every damn day.

Today Is Tomorrow's Yesterday

Here's my challenge to you in this fall season of whiskey stupidity and spite. Take five minutes out of your day. Sit down with a pencil and paper and write down the ten whiskeys that matter most to you. Why ten? It's just a start. You can write more or less. That's up to you. When you're done, take that list and review your cabinet. Is it an honest list, or did you merely write down whiskeys you think you want? In other words, is what's on your list reflective of what's actually sitting in your cabinet—opened, enjoyed, appreciated? If not, I encourage you to sit back down and be truthful. Only then will you be ready for step two.

In that very same cabinet (better yet, a completely separate one), set aside space for each of the bottles on your list. Let's call this space your "whiskey time capsule." Each time you visit your local store, buy one of those bottles on your list along with whatever else you were originally planning to purchase. Each time you return home from these trips, place your listed bottle in your whiskey time capsule. Important: if you run out of a specific listed expression that's a regular of yours, *don't open your time capsule bottle.* Just pick up another the next time you're out shopping and *leave your whiskey time capsule alone.*

Now, some might call this idea unoriginal. Some may say it's simply a bunker. No. This isn't a stockpile of highly allocated or overhyped releases. This isn't a "tater hoard" or combustible investment. *This is your whiskey time capsule:* one bottle of each of the whiskeys you enjoy on a regular

MY WHISKEY TIME CAPSULE

_____
_____
_____
_____
_____
_____
_____
_____
_____
_____
_____
_____
_____
_____
_____
_____

basis *right now*. When you complete your checklist, shut the cabinet, or isolate that particular section off completely. Let the years go by . . . five, ten, maybe even fifteen or twenty years. You now have the ability to literally travel back in whiskey time. Open a bottle with an old friend, or maybe a son or daughter that's come of age. Celebrate one of life's milestones with a vintage expression you once tucked away effortlessly at retail price. Who knows? Whiskey might be in bad shape by the time you finally explore your time capsule. Supply and demand are fickle things, as are the trends that fuel them. And then there's legislation and regulations that could change everything. You just never know.

I'm not saying you should be a "whiskey prepper." I'm just saying we're living in the Great Whiskey Dynasty. Why stress your life out over the same old seasonal allocated bottles when you have quality bourbon and rye right down the street? Excellent whiskey is virtually everywhere, and Wild Turkey is arguably the best place to start looking for it. But you don't have to take my word for it. Get out there and do your thing. Buy and sip what speaks to you most, and as you do, try your best to never take that whiskey for granted.

RICKHOUSE BLUES

Rickhouse Blues

Born out of frustration with poorly labeled Wild Turkey single-barrel expressions, "Rickhouse Blues" laid out my arguments addressing the matter. To this day, I still field emails and social media inquiries from confused and confounded whiskey enthusiasts seeking to learn precisely where a given barrel was aged. Hopefully, by the time you're reading this book, the issue has been resolved. Perhaps bottle labels and tags will finally disclose thorough and accurate information. If so, hallelujah! If not, this post maintains its unfortunate relevance. dj

SEPTEMBER 29, 2020

Recently, one question has been asked of me more than any other: "How do I know if my Wild Turkey single-barrel whiskey is from Tyrone or Camp Nelson?" I try to answer as best I can, based on the limited knowledge I have (I'm not a Wild Turkey employee, after all). Unfortunately, my responses are never guaranteed to be 100 percent accurate. Regardless of which rickhouses are in season annually (or applicable to a specific year's single barrel program), in theory *any barrel could be pulled from any rickhouse from any campus*: Tyrone, Camp Nelson, or McBrayer. Also, barrels are occasionally moved from one campus to another, such is the case with many rickhouse Q-, S-, and T-labeled single-barrel bottlings (potentially others as well).

Before we dive into this subject, I should first stress why it's important. Provenance. It's a whiskey enthusiast's rock. Knowing what you're sipping, who made it, and where it came from matters. And for Wild Turkey, it matters more than most Kentucky distilleries. Whereas many producers rely on multiple mash bills and yeasts to achieve unique profiles, Wild Turkey has only a single bourbon and rye recipe, each sharing the same yeast. When you exclude the barrel-entry proof changes from the mid-2000s and the new distillery launched into service in 2011, the only factor contributing to profile variance is maturation. Sure, different distillation runs might equate to some subtleties in new make. But with computerized automation in place, the range of that variance is arguably minimal.

Going back to the start of Wild Turkey's first single-barrel product in 1994, Kentucky Spirit's label provided consumers with two pieces of information relative to each bottling's aging location: rickhouse (labeled as "warehouse") and rack (labeled as "rick"). Sparse disclosure continued through the 1990s and 2000s with Kentucky Legend and Wild Turkey Heritage, both of which were duty-free, single-barrel releases. In that time, Wild Turkey had acquired Camp Nelson and its six rickhouses. It was also leasing space in the stone rickhouses of the former Old Taylor Distillery (now Castle & Key). As for McBrayer, which was acquired in 1976 from Four Roses, space was growing limited due to deterioration and safety concerns. Still, consumers had only a rickhouse letter and a rack to go by.

In 2013, a new Wild Turkey single-barrel expression hit retail shelves: Russell's Reserve Single Barrel Bourbon. Sadly, no maturation information was stated on its label: no barrel number, no rickhouse, no floor, no rack, no age, no dates. Nada. Believe it or not, it's still that way (thank goodness we at least have bottle codes). It was followed by Russell's Reserve Single Barrel Rye in 2015, but unfortunately, still no maturation details. There was one exception, however: the barrels bottled for the private selection program.

By 2014, distributors and retailers were given the opportunity to select their own unique Wild Turkey barrels, which could then be bottled as Kentucky Spirit (bourbon) or Russell's Reserve Single Barrel (bourbon or rye). These selections included tags situated around the neck of the bottle. At first the tags were filled out by hand (c. 2015) but later printed as the program progressed (c. 2016). These tags provided a barrel number, rickhouse, floor, and the name of the party or company that participated in the selection. In 2017, the rack and row/position information were included with the floor number, though dates and campus remained omitted.

PROVENANCE.

IT'S A WHISKEY ENTHUSIAST'S ROCK. KNOWING WHAT YOU'RE SIPPING, WHO MADE IT, AND WHERE IT CAME FROM MATTERS.

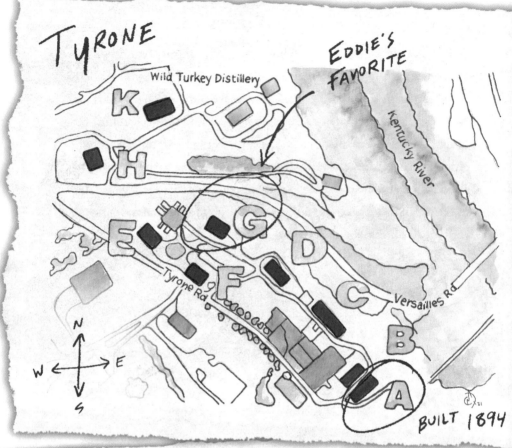

TYRONE

EDDIE'S FAVORITE

Wild Turkey Distillery

K

D

H

Kentucky River

E

G

D

Tyrone Rd

F

C

Versailles Rd

B

N
W — E
S

A

BUILT 1894

Wild Turkey Distillery

S   O   N

W

X

Q

M

Y

V

Kentucky River

R

P

Z

T

U

N
W — E
S

J   BURNED IN 2000

Camp Nelson

D   C   E

A   B   F

Kentucky River

FORMER SITE OF
CANADA DRY BOURBON

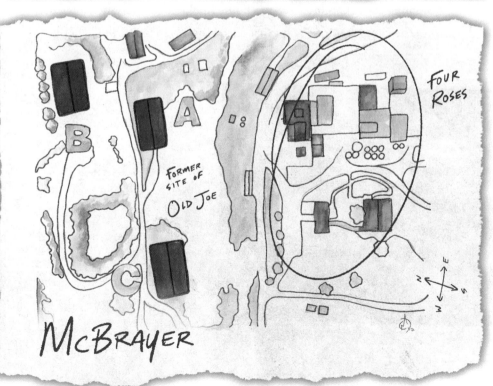

B   A

FORMER SITE OF
OLD JOE

C

FOUR ROSES

McBrayer

Then came 2018, and a curious new set of letters found their way onto private selection tags: "CN." Ah, Camp Nelson. Virtually unknown to most whiskey enthusiasts at the time (including Wild Turkey geeks like myself), it didn't take long for Camp Nelson to garner significant buzz. Why? Because the flavor profiles fans were experiencing stood out from years prior, particularly in relation to Russell's Reserve Single Barrel Bourbon. Almost overnight, location meant more than ever. It was an exciting time for fans of Wild Turkey, the momentum carrying on through 2019, which I often refer to as "The Year of Camp Nelson."

And then it happened. The big change. What should've been a resounding improvement for Wild Turkey's single barrel program resulted in (yet another) frustrating mess. Of course, I'm referring to the removal of hang tags and the introduction of a new private selection label for Russell's Reserve Single Barrel Bourbon in mid/late 2019.

Dammit.

I'm sorry, I needed to get that out. But seriously, if you're going to do something, do it right. As much as I love and appreciate barrel information becoming permanently affixed to a bottle (including important dates), why omit the campus information that enthusiasts were so thrilled about the year prior? Buzz killed.

And here we are in 2020. If a Russell's Reserve or Kentucky Spirit label states A, B, C, D, E, or F, we don't know for certain if that's Tyrone or Camp Nelson. Not to mention, I have no clue how McBrayer rickhouse barrels are labeled. (There can't be more than two or three.) I can only assume alpha designations like the others (so A, B, C?). Yet it bears repeating that this information means something to whiskey enthusiasts. It should matter to non-enthusiast consumers as well. If someone purchases a single-barrel selection and loves the profile, they might just make note of the aging location and search for a similar bottle. (I hope it's not a bottle labeled "A." If so, good luck.)

At this point, I think it's pretty clear why fans of Wild Turkey need campus information on single-barrel bottlings. Now, I'm going to give Campari a little incentive.

Imagine a product that encourages consumers to purchase a set or series. Much like a baseball card collector who seeks out missing cards, whiskey consumers desire a complete collection. What drives that desire is slightly different for the individual, yet it exists. And I can tell you for a fact it exists for Wild Turkey fans. We want to experience every rickhouse Wild Turkey owns. We want to taste, share, discuss, and compare every single one. Hell, there are countless folks already trying to obtain a bottle from each. They want the entire series. As is, Campari is leaving money on the table. Were every single-barrel product labeled accurately, sales would likely increase. By the volume of inquiries I receive, I'd bank on it.

Wrapping up, I'd like to circle back to something I stated a few paragraphs back. If you're going to do something, do it right. If a consumer is curious in which rickhouse a particular Russell's Reserve Single Barrel or Kentucky Spirit matured, they look to the label for an answer. The sheer fact they have to follow that up with a second (often unanswered) question is a failure. When someone asks me where I grew up, I don't answer with just "Carolina." If I did, it would only confuse or frustrate the inquirer. At best they'd ask for clarification of North or South. At worst they'd assume I don't care for them to know. It's communication 101.

There's enough confusion and frustration in whiskey these days. In the grand scheme of things, Wild Turkey is a minor offender. It's annoying, easy-to-fix items like this that keep it on the radar. Let's fix it.

Bittersweet & Bold: The Old Fashioned Cocktail

Who doesn't love a good Old Fashioned? If you don't, maybe you just haven't tried the right one.

By the Fall of 2020, I was enjoying cocktails more than ever. COVID-19 stay-at-home measures led to a greater appreciation of the craft. I certainly didn't consider myself a mixologist after just eight months, or even a drink-slinger in training, but I liked exploring new avenues with whiskey.

The Old Fashioned is a cocktail ripe for experimentation, as its core ingredients are simple and sparse. Keep your cocktail whiskey-focused and it's hard to go wrong. Besides, I'm certain there are a few bottles in your cabinet needing attention. That's a good place to start! dj

NOVEMBER 17, 2020

There are few cocktails that capture my interest like the Old Fashioned. Simple, classic, delicious . . . all appropriate adjectives to describe it. But long before *Mad Men*'s Don Draper heralded its twenty-first century revival, the Old Fashioned occupied glasses of the restless and thirsty since 1880 (and well before then, many mixologists and historians argue).

Like a majority of cocktails, the Old Fashioned is part sweet, part bitter. The key is finding balance between the two, and it all starts with the base spirit. While history tells us Old Fashioned cocktails were sometimes crafted with gin or brandy, modern iterations rely primarily on whiskey, specifically bourbon or rye whiskey. One is always welcome to craft an Old Fashioned with Scotch, Irish, or Japanese whiskey, that's just not me. I much prefer bourbon or rye; moreover, I prefer it with Jimmy Russell's amber Kentucky elixir, Wild Turkey.

Which brings me to the first of three Old Fashioned cocktail recipes I'd like to share with you today, my personal house Old Fashioned.

RARE BIRD 101 OLD FASHIONED

* 1 ounce Wild Turkey 101 Bourbon
* 1 ounce Wild Turkey 101 Rye
* ½ tsp simple syrup
* 2 dashes Angostura bitters
* 2 dashes Peychaud's bitters

In a rocks glass, combine ½ teaspoon simple syrup with 2 dashes Angostura bitters and 2 dashes Peychaud's bitters; add 1 ounce Wild Turkey 101 Bourbon and 1 ounce Wild Turkey 101 Rye; fill the glass with ice (or a large ice cube/sphere) and stir; garnish with a lemon slice and a cocktail cherry.

What I like most about this recipe is that it showcases the harmony that can be achieved between bourbon and rye via cocktail. There's a fair number of bourbon-rye (or "bourye") whiskeys out there. Wild Turkey had its own with Forgiven. Unfortunately, bourbon and rye blends don't work as well as people often expect (particularly with Wild Turkey). In other words, the sum isn't always as great as the parts. Cocktails are another story, however. One has the luxury of sweet elements, like sugar or simple syrup, and various bitters to glue the occasionally opposing spirits together.

In the case of my house Old Fashioned, and with most of my cocktails, simple syrup is kept to a minimum. (I find both Wild Turkey 101 and Wild Turkey 101 Rye to be sweet enough neat.) As for the bitters, I prefer an even measure of Angostura and Peychaud's. The Angostura provides the typical bitter aromatics, while the Peychaud's contrasts with a touch of delicate fruitiness. Garnishing with a cocktail cherry and a ripe lemon slice enhances the overall sweet/zesty balance and helps to maintain flavor as the ice melts.

Pineapple Old Fashioned

* 2 ¼ ounces Wild Turkey Rye*
* 3 teaspoons pineapple juice
* ½ teaspoon sugar
* 2 dashes Angostura bitters

In a rocks glass, combine 3 teaspoons pineapple juice with ½ teaspoon granulated sugar (stir until dissolved); add 2 dashes Angostura bitters and 2 ¼ ounces Wild Turkey Rye; fill the glass with ice and stir; garnish with a pineapple slice and a maraschino cherry.

Though I consider this cocktail more of a summertime treat, it has its place in the winter holiday season. Fruitcake and pineapple cake are each popular this time of year, so why not enjoy a pineapple-based beverage? Hell, it might just make Uncle Larry's same old yarns a bit more tolerable. And with an 81-proof spirit base, you might appreciate more than one.

(Who am I kidding? Of course, you will!) But seriously, the lower-proof rye works great in this combination. Think of it as a Pineapple Mimosa, but with whiskey instead of champagne. (Please don't judge my logic.)

*Substitution: If the 81-proof Wild Turkey Rye is unavailable, use 2 ounces of Wild Turkey 101 Rye and a splash of water instead.

MY OLD FASHIONED RECIPE:

TITLE HERE
_____

_____
_____
_____
_____
_____
_____
_____
_____
_____
_____
_____
_____
_____
_____
_____
_____

PHOTO HERE

THE DON VALDEZ

* 1 large coffee ice cube/sphere (unsweetened)
* 2 ounces Russell's Reserve Single Barrel Bourbon
* ½ teaspoon simple syrup
* 2 dashes black walnut bitters
* 1 dash Angostura bitters

Place one large unsweetened coffee ice cube/sphere in a rocks glass; pour 2 ounces Russell's Reserve Single Barrel Bourbon over the ice; add ½ teaspoon simple syrup, 2 dashes black walnut bitters, and 1 dash Angostura bitters; stir generously; garnish with an expressed orange peel and a cocktail cherry.

While my house Old Fashioned is a regular favorite, given the right day a "Don Valdez" might just take its place. What's a Don Valdez? It's a play on words: a combination of the enigmatic Don Draper and coffee legend Juan Valdez. Essentially, a Don Valdez is an Old Fashioned cocktail with a coffee twist, though it's important to note that the coffee is introduced solely in the form of ice.

Perhaps the most surprising thing about this recipe is how the seemingly unconventional element (in this case coffee) works so well with the conventional ones. In fact, the only ingredient that truly stands out as unique is the coffee. While you can choose to make your ice out of whichever coffee blend or brew you wish, an unsweetened cold brew (such as Stok) works best.

Also, I recommend using Russell's Reserve Single Barrel Bourbon over Wild Turkey Bourbon or Wild Turkey 101. I find Russell's 110 proof is ideal, considering the generous stirring needed to introduce the coffee to the spirit (it also keeps the drink spirit-forward). The black walnut bitters only accent the coffee's flavor, while the Angostura reminds you that you're sipping an Old Fashioned (not some trendy FrankenFrapp). When garnishing, be sure to express the orange peel, as the oil helps to offset the darker/nuttier notes imparted by the coffee and black walnut bitters.

And there you have it—three completely different, yet equally flavorful Old Fashioned cocktails. If you're a traditionalist, stick with my house recipe. But if you're in search of a little adventure, give the Pineapple Old Fashioned or Don Valdez a shot. Call me biased, but I think you'll love all three. Whatever you do, please don't feel bound to these recipes. As with whiskey, the perfect drink is relative to the individual. You decide what works and what doesn't. And if you find something that works better (a different method, element substitution, etc.), feel free to shoot me an email or send a direct message on social media. I'd love to hear your thoughts. Until then, Cheers!

THE BEST OF 2020

The Best of 2020

Was there anything good about 2020? Actually, yes. In a year full of social and political strife, economic meltdown, and the largest pandemic in over a century, Wild Turkey delivered a slate of quality releases: Rare Breed Rye, Master's Keep Bottled in Bond, Russell's Reserve 2003, and, for the first time in over a year, Tyrone aged Russell's Reserve Single Barrel private selections. These releases didn't solve the world's problems, but they damn sure relieved stress and gave Wild Turkey fans something to look forward to.

Looking back, I view 2020 as a turning point for Wild Turkey. The "New Golden Age" became a reality, as oblivious consumers and diehard enthusiasts alike had apparently been living in denial. New expressions, particularly Master's Keep Bottled in Bond, were no longer destined to collect dust on liquor store shelves. In fact, in some locales, bottles were sold before they could even be tagged. Eyes were opened, the flames of interest were stoked, and things would never be the same for Wild Turkey. dj

December 8, 2020

I t's that time of year again—time for my annual "Best of" post. I'm sure you've already seen enough 2020 retrospective whiskey lists to make your eyes cross, but mine's all Wild Turkey! And what's not to love about Wild Turkey? So, without further ado, I give you 2020's best.

Best Design (2020)
Russell's Reserve 2003

While a contender for Best Whiskey Overall, I wrestle with the fact this rare bourbon was severely allocated and expensive ($250 suggested retail price). As a result, very few Turkey fans were able to find, much less afford Russell's Reserve 2003. But regardless of ownership or whether or not one had the opportunity to taste it, there's one thing we can all appreciate: it's damn sure easy on the eyes.

Similar to past Russell's Reserve limited editions, such as 1998 and 2002, Russell's Reserve 2003 is housed in a brand-appropriate, spartan wood box. The bottle itself is essentially the standard Russell's Reserve squat glass; however, the metal logo/seal and neckband give it a rustic luxurious touch. Its label, while minimal in design, provides all of the details a whiskey geek should want. It also gives 2003 more of a hand-crafted look, despite its apparent manufactured origin.

Yet, the real star of the show is the whiskey. Thankfully, Russell's Reserve 2003's minimalist aesthetics provide sufficient space for the mature, barrel-proof bourbon to shine through. We've seen this feature in past Campari designs, like Master's Keep and Longbranch, and I hope to see more of it in the years to come. In fact, if I had my way, this is the type of design (sans box) I'd employ with the upcoming Russell's Reserve 13-Year. That would require another TTB filing, however. But I can be patient. How about it, Campari?

BEST CORE EXPRESSION (2020)
WILD TURKEY RARE BREED
(BATCH 116.8)

Barrel-proof bourbon expressions from major distilleries aren't hard to find nowadays, but that wasn't always the case. Jim Beam kicked off the trend with Booker's in 1988, with Wild Turkey's Rare Breed following shortly after in 1991. Both Booker's and Rare Breed remain regularly produced expressions for their relative brands, yet the pricing between the two has grown substantially. Once priced similarly, Rare Breed is, at $45, now half the price of Booker's (sometimes less than half, retailer depending). Neither have changed their reported maturations or specifications, yet Rare Breed maintains its working-class price.

Here we are in 2020, and the competition is fiercer than ever with releases such as Maker's Mark Cask Strength, Bulleit Barrel Strength, Elijah Craig Barrel Proof, and so on. Even so, Rare Breed has complexity, affordability, and most importantly, availability. Finding another barrel-proof bourbon with all three of these aspects isn't so easy. And while I've never had a Rare Breed 116.8 to disappoint, 2020's batches are some of the bests I've ever tasted. But don't just take my word for it. There are countless writers, bloggers, Redditors, and YouTubers that feel the same. If you've yet to try Rare Breed batch 116.8, you're missing out.

WILD TURKEY RARE BREED RYE
(BATCH 112.2)

Another contender for Best Whiskey overall, Wild Turkey delivered its first jab square on the nose of 2020 with Rare Breed Rye. Reportedly a blend of four-, six-, and eight-year rye whiskey, Rare Breed Rye is Wild Turkey's first ever barrel-proof rye (bottled non-chill filtered, to boot). Talk about flavor! It's everything one loves about Wild Turkey 101 Rye "cranked to eleven": vanilla candy, caramel drizzle, lemon squares, zesty citrus, faint mint, and loads of peppery spice. I honestly don't think one could come up with a better rye iteration to bear the Rare Breed name. A damn fine job, Mr. Russell.

Let's hope we see increased distribution of Rare Breed Rye in 2021. Wild Turkey's rye stocks are significantly less than its bourbon stocks and have been for years, but production has ramped up over the last decade.

Based on the reported ages of this expression, I'm thinking we'll see this hanging around on shelves a bit longer by 2022. It's just an educated guess, so I'll keep my fingers crossed for now.

BEST SINGLE BARREL (2020)
RUSSELL'S RESERVE SINGLE BARREL BOURBON
(#20-1209, LINCOLN ROAD PACKAGE STORE)

It may not be the best single barrel I've tasted in my life, and surely not the highest I've rated on my blog, but what Lincoln Road's #20-1209 lacks in specs and exclusivity, it more than makes up for in satisfaction. The last time I enjoyed a private selection in this same manner was Justins' House of Bourbon's #18-708 . . . flavorful and fun! Simply put, there's excitement in Jamie Farris's unassuming eight-year selection from Tyrone A—caramel apple, vanilla frosting, zesty fruit, and earthy spice. It's unbelievably balanced, impressing me each time I pour a glass.

There's a lesson in this bottle, and I'm reminded of Reid & Emerald's famous six-year 1789b Willett Family Estate #797 (damn, was that good): when it comes to straight whiskey, age is only a number. In a year with so many fantastic ten- and eleven-year Wild Turkey single barrels (several of which I debated for this award); it might surprise folks that I elected Lincoln Road's #20-1209. While those well-aged barrels are excellent, there's something special about a profile you keep coming back to over and over again. It's not easily explained, but regardless of age, when it's right, it's right. Oh, and if you're looking for a private selection compass, give Jamie and Misty Farris a call.

PATRON'S CHOICE (2020)
RUSSELL'S RESERVE SINGLE BARREL BOURBON

Last year, I asked my generous Patreon supporters to select a Wild Turkey expression they felt deserving of praise. They elected Campari's W.B. Saffell, and I don't blame them one bit. This year, out of the sea of annual Wild Turkey expressions, they chose another personal favorite of mine, Russell's Reserve Single Barrel Bourbon. Once again, I don't blame them.

What can be said about Russell's Reserve Single Barrel that hasn't been said already? When it comes to tasting whiskey straight from a unique Wild Turkey barrel, outside of occasional Single Cask Nation bottlings, this is as close as you'll get to the real thing.

Bottled non-chill filtered at 110 proof, Russell's Reserve Single Barrel is only five points away from Wild Turkey's 115 barrel-entry proof. It's typically aged eight to ten years and is closely supervised by Eddie Russell himself. Not to mention you get a quality variance straight from Mother Nature that's unlike any other Kentucky distillery. Whereas many producers rely on multiple mash bills and yeasts to achieve variance, Wild Turkey's single bourbon recipe blossoms into exceptional profiles thanks to traditional wood/clad rickhouses situated on multiple campuses.

If you're looking for a one-of-a-kind single-barrel bourbon of the highest quality without driving around town or spending ridiculous money, Russell's Reserve Single Barrel Bourbon is the best place to start. And you won't have to seek out a private selection to find a winner. If you think about it, every Russell's Reserve Single Barrel is an Eddie selection. I think it's safe to say that fella knows what he's doing.

WILD TURKEY MASTER'S KEEP BOTTLED IN BOND

I think we can all agree, as bad a year as 2020 has been, it's been a solid year for Wild Turkey expressions. And if there's one 2020 release that surely deserves accolades, it's Master's Keep Bottled in Bond. On paper alone, this one is impressive. Aged seventeen years at the Camp Nelson rickhouses in Jessamine County, bottled in bond and batched under the guidance of Eddie Russell, Master's Keep Bottled in Bond is a perfect example of what a limited edition should be: a unique, notably aged whiskey with unquestionable provenance.

As for Master's Keep Bottled in Bond's flavor profile, it's very much what 2018's Russell's Reserve 2002 should've been—similar Camp Nelson attributes, yet refined, balanced, and slightly sweeter. And the oak influence . . . toasted cherry, antique leather, cedar, fragrant dry spice . . . complex, layered, lovely. One could nose this whiskey all evening! Upon tasting, any concerns that a similar elegance shouldn't proceed to the palate and finish are quickly dismissed. Dare I say the elegance is only enhanced?

There are few bourbons showcasing such grace and enjoyability at seventeen years of age—hell, even some at twelve years of age. To do so, and have it where enthusiasts can find it and afford it as a special occasion purchase, is remarkable. I'm not sure that Wild Turkey can keep that going forever, however. As whiskey enthusiasm grows, the undeserved myth that Wild Turkey is a roughneck's bourbon fades. It's a positive thing for the brand, and a hard-fought achievement for the Russells, no doubt. But the time is upon us when releases like this won't linger on retailers' shelves. Gone are the days when Wild Turkey limited editions were the punchline of "shelf turd" jokes. (We'll leave that torch with you, Woodford.)

Jokes aside, we're truly living in the New Golden Age of Wild Turkey. Savor it. Share it. And cheers to Jimmy, Eddie, and the hardworking folks at Wild Turkey and Campari for making all of this possible.

Wild Turkey Father & Son and the Fear of Missing Out

The things people do for a fast buck!

I'd been aware of Wild Turkey Father & Son for at least a year before I finally tasted it. Frankly, it didn't seem like a bottle I needed to chase. I'd tasted thirteen-year Wild Turkey before and tracking down duty-free expressions is no walk in the park (especially when international travel is severely restricted). Nevertheless, an opportunity presented itself in early 2021, so I jumped. I'm glad I did.

And then began the secondary whiskey market cash-grab . . .

I have nothing more to add to what I said in February of 2021, though I still feel as strongly. As it would turn out, a second supply of Father & Son would be retailed via the same online vendor in April 2021 (additional supply followed). They didn't last long and, of course, were instantly flipped the following day. Interestingly, the secondary market premium dropped 35 percent from the months preceding. Still, it was a ridiculous premium considering the suggested retail price. I just hope that Wild Turkey fans who missed out the first time were able to secure a reasonably priced bottle at some point. dj

FEBRUARY 17, 2021

I prefer a little time before writing a formal review of a new Wild Turkey release. Unfortunately, some recent secondary-market shenanigans have spurred me to share my feelings a bit early regarding the new travel-retail exclusive, Wild Turkey Father & Son.

What is Father & Son? It's a thirteen-year, 86-proof Kentucky straight bourbon bottled as a liter and sold at select travel-retail outlets. No thanks/thanks to COVID-19, things didn't go exactly as planned, and an unknown number of Father & Son cases landed in the hands of a European distributor. Many of those bottles were later sold on Must Have Malts, a reputable online retailer, and the rest, as they say, is history.

I was fortunate enough to purchase a bottle for 65 Euros (about $79). A liter-worth of thirteen-year Wild Turkey bourbon is surely worth that price, not to mention the exclusivity, fancy packaging, etc. to give it additional appeal. Of course, there's the expense of overseas shipping and handling. Such is the world we live in. But to be completely honest, I initially hesitated on pulling the trigger. After all, the 90-proof Russell's Reserve 10-Year is right down the street for $35. Based on my experience with the Japanese thirteen-year Distiller's Reserve, those profiles are comparable. I reasoned Father & Son would repeat that observation, possibly even taking a step down at 86 proof.

Spoiler: I was wrong.

But, before reaching for your iPhone to scour the secondary, I think it's important to read this entire post. I have much to say about Father & Son, as well as the state of the bourbon marketplace today. I'll stop right here and jump to my tasting notes. Besides, I'm going to need a drink with all that I have to say.

Wild Turkey Father & Son — "Jimmy & Eddie Russell's Choice"

SPIRIT:	Kentucky straight bourbon whiskey
PROOF:	86
AGE:	thirteen years
MISC.:	distilled and bottled by Wild Turkey Distilling Co., Lawrenceburg, KY; supplied for Campari Australia Pty Ltd
	tasted neat in a Glencairn Glass after a few minutes rest...
COLOR:	amber
NOSE:	(mature, woody) fragrant oak, medicinal cherry, leather, potpourri, apple-cinnamon, heady dark citrus, and honeysuckle
TASTE:	(thin, yet velvety mouthfeel) toasted vanilla, English toffee, earthy spice (licorice, sassafras, clove), cherry pie, hints of grapefruit
FINISH:	medium long, oak-laden finish—burnt honey, black tea, spiced oak char, dry herbs, diminishing leather, and cracked pepper

OVERALL:

I'm sincerely impressed. Wild Turkey Father & Son is excellent; more importantly, it steers free from repeating the profile of the thirteen-year Distiller's Reserve. This is most definitely its own bourbon, and a distinctly mature and fine bourbon at that.

Maybe I'm off, but I highly doubt there's only thirteen-year whiskey in Father & Son. Come to think of it, it tastes pretty damn close to the seventeen-year Master's Keep Bottled in Bond. Father & Son may not be as robust or captivating, but for an 86-proof whiskey, it sure as hell gets my attention—promptly.

If you can find Wild Turkey Father & Son for retail price (or there-abouts), it's a definite buy. At least, it earns my recommendation. This is undoubtedly a special whiskey—one that will make you appreciate the complexity Wild Turkey can achieve at a lower proof with the right barrels. Father & Son is what Master's Keep 1894 should've been. I just hope our Aussie sisters and brothers can find it. They deserve it.

FEAR & FOLLY

As mentioned in my introduction, it's come to my attention that Wild Turkey Father & Son hit secondary markets immediately after it was listed on Must Have Malts. I've seen screenshots of individuals asking $380. Then it rose to $450. Where it's at now, I can't say. But I can say this: please don't pay hundreds of dollars for this bourbon. It's simply not worth it. At best, it's a notch above Diamond Anniversary. It's not quite Master's Keep Decades level, and it's certainly not Master's Keep Bottled in Bond or Russell's Reserve 2003. I believe all of those, save for maybe Russell's Reserve 2003, can be found for much less than $450.

The state of the bourbon secondary market is ridiculous. Each day I hear about certain MGP-distilled non-distiller producer (or "NDP") releases, like Smoke Wagon, selling for entirely unreasonable amounts of money. That's right, MGP, who pumps out whiskey like a well-oiled machine. It's great whiskey, but nothing rare. And let's not forget Buffalo Trace. At this point, I'm convinced Buffalo Trace could release distilled water in a Blanton's bottle and it would be allocated. It's not Buffalo Trace's fault, but the lengths people will go to acquire horsey-topped, non-age-stated, 93-proof mediocre bourbon is astounding. And now (sigh) . . . Wild Turkey.

Forget Pappy. Forget BTAC. Forget Birthday Bourbon. All you need to make tons of money on the secondary is a black magic known as FOMO.

The "fear of missing out" is a powerful thing. It drives. It haunts. It leads to irrational thought, and more often than not, profound buyer's remorse. I'm just as guilty of it, as are many of you reading, and not only with bourbon but many things in life. But, as you get older or just more experienced in your particular realm of interest—in this case, whiskey— you begin to see the error of your ways. More so than that, you realize that there are people out there willing to capitalize on your fear. They have no interest other than making a fast buck. Some even resort to counterfeiting bottles. This is the unfortunate side of our hobby.

Some of you might be thinking, "It's just supply and demand. The market is what it is." And to that I'll respond with, I get it. But that doesn't mean the secondary market represents our hobby well. Sure, there are legitimate licensed entities (specialty shops, auction houses, etc.) that sell whiskeys (particularly vintage bottles) outside of the typical retail marketplace. They guard the consumer, guarantee their product, and provide safe ways to acquire hard-to-find bottles. I'm supportive and grateful they're around. But when Joe Monday snags an exclusive bottle (a bottle he's never even tasted) off a foreign website for $79, then instantly flips it (not even in-hand) for four or five times its retail price, that's more than being opportunistic. It's exploitative. It's precisely what we don't need.

Yet, we let it carry on. We enable it. Like it or not, if this practice of exorbitant flipping continues, someone or some authority will clean it up (possibly forever). It's probably best if that cleanup starts with us, sooner than later. I don't have the answers, but I don't believe secondary markets are as healthy for this industry as some propose. I'm sure it gives producers a high to see their expressions valued multiple times over their retail prices. But that high only lasts so long. It eventually turns into expectation and desire, followed by a realization that their products are apparently (severely, yet artificially) underpriced.

In the end, whiskey flippers hurt consumers and we pay for it—even the ones who avoid it. One way or another, we all pay for this behavior. And frankly, I don't see it changing. Pandora's Blanton's box is open. At best we can watch out for our close friends, associates, and those within our whiskey clubs and social groups. Whenever we see this type of behavior, call it out and ask that it be shut down. You may place yourself in a position to lose your membership, but if that's the case, maybe it's a group you shouldn't trouble yourself with anyway. Maybe they don't have your best interest in mind. Of course, that's a call you'll have to make.

I'll close with this. If whiskey enthusiasm means more to you than money, that is if discovering, sharing, and finding common ground with your fellow enthusiast is what you're in this for, avoid the flippers. They couldn't be further apart from your passion and integrity.

Stay safe and look out for one another. Please.

THE FEAR OF MISSING OUT IS A POWERFUL THING. IT DRIVES. IT HAUNTS. IT LEADS TO IRRATIONAL THOUGHT, AND MORE OFTEN THAN NOT, PROFOUND BUYER'S REMORSE.

THE ESSENCE OF
EDDIE RUSSELL

The Essence of Eddie Russell

Shortly after writing "The Essence of Jimmy Russell" in September of 2019, I knew the day would come when I'd pen a similar post for Eddie. That day just happened to be Eddie Russell's birthday.

Some blog posts, particularly reviews, take days to flesh out. Truthfully, I had another piece written for March 30, 2021. But, as I sat down to share my thoughts on what I assumed would be a brief social media "happy birthday" post, I quickly realized I had a lot more to say about the talented Mr. Russell. In a few hours, "The Essence of Eddie Russell" was complete.

It's uncommon to finish an article so quickly. When I do, they're typically fueled by emotion. Writing about the Russells is never a dull venture; I could talk for hours on end (and have before) about their accomplishments and importance to Wild Turkey, its legacy, and fans. Many people know about Jimmy Russell and should. Yet, Eddie Russell has achieved what very few can—making a near-equivalent mark on a brand so strongly tied to a living legend.

You've come a long way, Eddie. This one's for you! dj

March 30, 2021

Today is Eddie Russell's birthday. How old is our favorite "new guy?" Old enough to make the best damn whiskey in the world. But you don't have to spend a fortune or waste hours of your day scrolling pages of shady internet secondary markets to appreciate some of Eddie's finest accomplishments. Sure, we'd all love to have his legendary Russell's Reserve 1998, but the probability of obtaining that bottle is bleak. As such, I thought I'd take a few minutes to share five Wild Turkey expressions that capture the essence of Kentucky Bourbon Hall-of-Famer Eddie Russell. The majority of these should be relatively easy to locate in some shape or form, ranging in price from $20 to $175. Not too bad considering modern-day whiskey prices.

Before I kick off the countdown, it's important to recognize Eddie Russell's significance to Wild Turkey. He's not Jimmy Russell. Never has been. Never claims to be. Yet, we all know Eddie has maintained the "heavy lifting" for some time, as Jimmy is well into his eighties. Frankly, Eddie deserves more credit than he receives from the general public. He'd never expect it nor ask for it. In fact, when speaking publicly, Eddie only casts the spotlight on his father. Jimmy and Eddie might not agree on everything (often don't), but there's a healthy and admirable level of respect one rarely finds outside of Kentucky's distilling families.

With that, let's review the last ten years—ten successful years—of Wild Turkey and highlight key expressions bearing Eddie Russell's influence. Many of these you'll find at your local bottle shop. Others may require a bit more searching, but they're out there. Either way, none should be priced too far above suggested retail. If they are, move along to another vendor. There's plenty of quality, appropriately priced Turkey to be found at reputable stores.

5. WILD TURKEY BOURBON (81 PROOF)

Some may disagree, but the old 80-proof Wild Turkey Bourbon is nothing to brag about. Some bottles are decent, others are just plain awful (literal drain pours). Quality aside, the inconsistency is astounding, and paying a premium for those 80-proof bottles—particularly releases from the 2000s—is not recommended. Why? It's been said that Jimmy Russell never liked making it, yet did so to satisfy a perceived niche in the market (and likely some suits in New York as well).

By 2011, Eddie Russell made it a priority to change this baseline expression, to turn it around and make it a noteworthy contender to its competition, like Jim Beam White Label and Jack Daniel's Old No.7. He accomplished the task by increasing the whiskey's maturity and proof. Whereas the old 80-proof expression was, in the words of Eddie, "four years and a day," the new 81-proof Wild Turkey Bourbon is crafted from whiskey aged five to eight years; essentially, a diluted, slightly younger Wild Turkey 101. Regarding the odd proof, the change from 80 to 81 merely signaled something was different, as well as riffing on the classic "1 over 100," in this case "1 over 80."

As for the whiskey's profile, I enjoy Wild Turkey Bourbon, or Wild Turkey 81 as it's sometimes called. It's better than Beam White or Jack Daniel's. It also works perfectly as a lower-proof summertime mixer in cola, ginger ale, or lemonade. The flavor on its own is nothing to gush about, but the expression and its origin story is. For $20, it's a solid Kentucky straight bourbon and a testament to Eddie Russell's drive to improve the Wild Turkey brand.

4. W.B. Saffell (Campari Whiskey Barons)

Campari's Whiskey Barons series was introduced in early 2017. The first two expressions, Old Ripy and Bond & Lillard (batch 1), performed moderately well, though probably not as well as Campari would have preferred. Some of that was due to the fact the Russells weren't involved, yet the press releases touted Wild Turkey bourbon as their primary source.

Whiskey enthusiasts are funny folk. We notice the small, tucked-away details. Combine that with a hefty price tag of $50 per 375ml, and one's motivation to purchase curious bottles isn't exactly spritely.

Then came 2019's W.B. Saffell. Word quickly spread about Eddie Russell's involvement and the rest is history. But it wasn't just the fact that Eddie proudly associated his name with the product. It was also the fact he fashioned an incredible tasting whiskey—so incredible that the $50 per 375ml meant very little to most bourbon fans. Many viewed it similar to paying $100 for a standard 750ml limited edition release. Hell, that's the way I saw it.

If you've yet to try W.B. Saffell, I encourage you to do so. Though a blend of bourbons aged six, eight, ten, and twelve years, it's rooted heavily around a ten-year profile. It's also a respectable 107 proof, falling between Wild Turkey 101 and Rare Breed, yet its robust and layered complexity sets it apart. Needless to say, a fantastic job by Eddie Russell, and a flavorful expression that I hope sticks around a little while longer.

3. Russell's Reserve Single Barrel Rye

In 2015, Eddie Russell was named master distiller, sharing the title with his famous father, of course. Perhaps it was a minor dose of rebellion, but Eddie's first core expression under his new title was Russell's Reserve Single Barrel Rye. Jimmy and Eddie may share a title, but they don't share a love for rye whiskey. If you've ever wondered why Wild Turkey rye was practically unheard of for sixty-plus years, it's because Jimmy's not a fan of rye whiskey. He can make it. He just doesn't like to sip it.

Eddie, on the other hand, was introduced to a new appreciation of rye largely because of his son, Bruce (now Brand Educator for Wild Turkey). Realizing there were some amazing rye barrels aging inconspicuously in some of their best rickhouses, he decided bottling these standouts at 104 proof (non-chill filtered) could provide whiskey enthusiasts a brand-new perspective on Wild Turkey's largely forgotten spirit. He was right.

Today, Russell's Reserve Single Barrel Rye remains an important part of Wild Turkey's portfolio. It's a fan favorite—one I keep on hand (and in my glass) regularly. It stands toe to toe with luxury rye offerings from other producers and does so for a fair $70. It may not be cheap, but it's considerably less expensive than other rye whiskeys of its maturity, quality, and class. It also tastes delicious.

2. Russell's Reserve Single Barrel Bourbon

At this point, I don't think there's an American whiskey enthusiast out there who's never heard of Russell's Reserve Single Barrel Bourbon. It wasn't always this way. Prior to 2013 and save for a handful of sparse travel-retail offerings, there was only one single-barrel Wild Turkey expression: Kentucky Spirit. At 101 proof, and bottled in a beautiful "fantail" glass, Kentucky Spirit was Jimmy Russell's baby. But Kentucky Spirit didn't capture the full-bodied, single-barrel sipping experience Eddie Russell felt it could.

The early 2010s saw shifts in Wild Turkey's general profile. This was primarily the result of barrel-entry proof changes instilled in 2004 and 2006. In order to capture the richness of sipping bourbon straight from a choice barrel, Wild Turkey needed a higher-proof single-barrel offering. 2013's Russell's Reserve Single Barrel Bourbon was the answer. With a 110-bottling proof, consumers could enjoy a full-flavored bourbon close to barrel strength, but at a consistent and generally approachable ABV. Bypassing chill filtration also helped, giving the bourbon greater mouthfeel and texture and, debatably, richer flavor.

The following year, Wild Turkey kicked off its private barrel program. Seven years later, it's skyrocketed in popularity. And rightfully so, as some of the most impressive whiskey bottled today can be found in Russell's Reserve Single Barrel private selections. The secret's out, folks. But it wouldn't be so if the bourbon didn't taste as remarkable as it does. We owe that to Eddie Russell.

EDDIE IS THE GUARDIAN, CUSTODIAN, AND SEASONED CARETAKER OF CLASSIC WILD TURKEY EXPRESSIONS LIKE WILD TURKEY 101, RARE BREED, AND RUSSELL'S RESERVE 10-YEAR.

1. WILD TURKEY MASTER'S KEEP (2015–PRESENT)

If you really want to understand Eddie Russell at his most bold and adventurous, give a Master's Keep expression a try. It doesn't matter which. Every enthusiast has their favorite for different reasons. Personally, with one rare exception (Master's Keep 1894), I'm a huge fan of them all. Now, I understand these aren't readily available for a number of you reading. Availability is relative to geographical location and marketplace. Some areas see these releases on shelves for weeks, months, even years; other areas, days or even hours (if out on shelves at all). The good news is there's more in the works, the next being Master's Keep One later this year.

What makes Master's Keep bold and adventurous? For starters, they're whiskeys Jimmy would likely never attempt. Jimmy's never been high on experimentation. He was trained by old-school distillers who believed in adherence to tradition and swore by consistency: do one thing, do it right, and don't change a damn thing, as they say. Conversely, Eddie is the product of a different generation. Growing up, he and his peers welcomed change and seldom shied from new things. They were high on experimentation (possibly other things at one time), breaking molds, pushing boundaries, and so on.

Master's Keep is Eddie Russell. His is the only name on every bottle—each an experiment in flavor, carefully crafted and meticulously supervised. I can't promise you'll love them all, but I can promise you'll appreciate the passion that went into them. Enjoy a hyper-mature bourbon? Try Master's Keep 17-Year or Master's Keep Bottled in Bond. Fancy a sherry-finished whiskey? Pick up Master's Keep Revival. So, you're a rye fan, eh? Check out Master's Keep Cornerstone. And last but not least, don't forget Master's Keep Decades. It may be the ultimate tribute to Eddie's tenure under his father, Jimmy.

Outside of the expressions listed above, Eddie is the guardian, custodian, and seasoned caretaker of classic Wild Turkey expressions like Wild Turkey 101, Rare Breed, and Russell's Reserve 10-Year, among so many others. As I've said, Eddie isn't Jimmy, but he's precisely the distiller Wild Turkey needs. Despite Jimmy's jests, in his heart I know he believes in "the new guy." He knows that no other could carry the flame better than Eddie. And we know it too.

Cheers to Eddie Russell! And have a very happy birthday, sir.

THE BEST WHISKEY IN THE WORLD

The Best Whiskey in the World

Pertinent, personal whiskey thoughts on my forty-fifth birthday. dj

JULY 31, 2021

Today is a day of reflection. Forty-five trips around the sun, many of which filled with satisfaction and joy, others, more difficult. Yet here I am. Alive. Breathing. I have my health. I have my friends and family. I have so much to be grateful for that I sometimes fear my priorities are misplaced. And, as whiskey enthusiasm skyrockets in popularity, those fears only intensify. I look around at rows and rows of bottles. Some mean more than others; some merely occupy space. What's all of this for? What am I seeking? These questions occasionally come to mind, as they most certainly have today.

I'm not going to bore you with a long existential sermon. I'm neither well-suited nor experienced enough to offer proven advice. But I would like to touch on one thing. In a hobby obsessed with the pursuit of the latest, greatest whiskey release, we haphazardly shift focus away from what matters most: our time.

Want to know a secret? The best whiskey in the world doesn't exist on the pages of elite Instagram influencers. It's not hiding in the backroom of your local bottle shop. It's in your cabinet right now. You possess the best whiskey in the world, and you may not even realize it.

Don't believe me? I didn't think you would. But don't write off my assertion just yet.

Go to your liquor cabinet and find your most reliable whiskey (I imagine it's front and center). It might be Wild Turkey 101 or Russell's Reserve 10-Year, or it might be Crown Royal or Jack Daniel's. It really doesn't matter. Grab a favorite everyday bottle and a glass and give yourself a healthy pour . . . hell, throw some ice or soda in the glass if that's how you roll. There's no drink shaming here.

Now, find a quiet place. Try stepping outside if the weather permits.

Sit. Close your eyes. Listen. Hear the sounds of the world around you.

Breathe. Take in the air and appreciate the fact that you can.

Settle your mind. Forget about the worries of the day or woes of society. This is your time—don't feel guilty taking it.

Slowly bring your glass to your nose. Take note of the scent. Consider the craftsmanship: the centuries of distilling knowledge passed down from generation to generation that made the whiskey in your hands possible.

Open your eyes and take a sip. Savor the spirit's flavor and the warmth of its finish. Breathe. At this moment, there's nothing but you and your whiskey. Your time. Your whiskey. The best whiskey in the world, dammit.

It's really that simple. Allocations, fancy bottles, rave reviews, secondary market bullshit are meaningless when it comes to what's truly best; nothing matters more than your time with your whiskey. Take that time. Cherish that time, as it's never guaranteed. There may never be a better whiskey than the one resting in your glass right now. Make it count.

The Best of 2021

How do I classify 2021? It was an odd year. Many assumed we'd see the end of the COVID-19 pandemic, and with it, life returning back to normal (I'll use that word loosely). That wasn't the case. If anything, 2021 felt more like a reboot of 2020. As *The Karate Kid*'s Mr. Miyagi puts it, "Different, but same."

But I'd be doing countless hardworking individuals a disservice if I said there wasn't improvement. In the bourbon world, distilleries were opening back up to the public—adjusting their protocols to keep visitors and employees safe. At Wild Turkey, brand builders like Bo Garrett hosted special onsite tastings with educational presentations. And though limited in number, there were even a few private barrel selections in the famed rickhouse A. All positive signs.

Sadly, things grew difficult for many retail consumers at home. Bottles once conveniently found—expressions like Russell's Reserve 10-Year and Rare Breed—were suddenly missing from store shelves. Some blamed an increased demand for premium whiskey, which certainly contributed to the shortage, but the reality had more to do supply issues, particularly with glass, and less to do with "bourbon mania."

It was in this climate that I set out to determine 2021's Best of Wild Turkey. Not that a lack of availability affected my decisions, but rather, knowing that

some enthusiasts were having difficulty acquiring even
the most common whiskeys on my list made it less celebratory. Thankfully, Wild Turkey has a proven history of
overcoming obstacles. This was 2021, but don't be surprised if the best is yet to come! dj

DECEMBER 31, 2021

L ove it or hate it, it's time for the inevitable year-end "top whiskey"
lists to flood social media. Not that it's necessarily a bad thing. Yes,
some are pure clickbait, even worse, paid promotions. But given an honest
perspective and a proper dose of substance, lists of annual favorites can be
informative and fun. At this point, my blog wouldn't be complete without
one. For the last four years, I've shared what I feel are the most noteworthy
Wild Turkey expressions: 2021 will prove no different.

BEST DESIGN (2021)
WILD TURKEY 101 / WILD TURKEY 101 RYE

To be completely accurate, the new Wild Turkey 101 (and 101 Rye) bottle
design first hit shelves in December of 2020, though it was only 1.75 liter
bottles (commonly known as "handles"). A few months down the road,
Wild Turkey formally launched the new "embossed Turkey" glass design
in multiple sizes: 750ml, 1 liter, as well as the aforementioned 1.75 liter.
Unfortunately, the spartan paper label 375ml bottle isn't much to brag
about, nor is the plastic 750ml "Traveler" bottle (frequently found in

2021 thanks to glass shortages), but I'm not including those (nor 50ml minis) in this award category.

What do I love most about the new embossed Turkey design? Primarily, it's simplistic elegance, though it's notably reminiscent of Wild Turkey 101 half-gallon bottles from the 1970s. As hot as vintage Wild Turkey is in 2021, it only makes sense that a semi-throwback design (whether intended or not) would be a hit with whiskey enthusiasts. That being said, not everyone is a fan. I've received numerous comments on social media wishing the new design never existed. I get it. Change isn't always an easy shot to swallow. But for me, at least in this case, it goes down smoother than Longbranch. Frankly, the embossed Turkey design is stellar, and I commend Campari for moving forward with it in a less-than-ideal year for change.

Best Core Expression (2021)
Russell's Reserve 10 Year Old Bourbon

Few whiskeys meet my lips as often as Russell's Reserve 10-Year. It's my modern-day rock—my go-to pour on any given day of the week (good or bad). Sadly, I've seen far less of it available in my area. While many speculate bourbon's meteoric rise in popularity as the primary culprit, I'm confident the issue has more to do with supply than demand. Not that there isn't a growing army of Russell's 10-Year fans out there. I see the love shared more and more each day. I just don't believe it's reached Eagle Rare or Henry McKenna 10-Year's status just yet.

As for why I love Russell's Reserve 10-Year so much—why it made this list—it's fairly straightforward. Russell's 10-Year checks virtually every box of what I'm looking for in a daily bourbon. It showcases a mature but easy-sipping flavorful profile. It's surprisingly affordable for its double-digit age statement. And it never lets me down. Whereas some whiskeys come and go or lean heavily on one's mood, Russell's 10-Year is always an appropriate pour. It may not be the perfect bourbon in a universal sense, but it's perfect enough for me.

BEST STRAIGHT RYE (2021)
WILD TURKEY RARE BREED RYE
(BATCH 112.2)

There's a hell of a lot of heavy-hitting rye whiskeys out there. That wasn't always the case. Rye whiskey's popularity may have shocked some, but certain veteran bartenders could've told you twenty years ago it was bound to happen. And here we are.

Let's face it, Wild Turkey is late to the barrel-proof rye game. It wasn't until 2020 when the Russells finally gave us what fans had been shouting for since Russell's Reserve Single Barrel Rye came onto the scene. And they answered with Rare Breed Rye.

This year, Rare Breed Rye once again wins my Best Straight Rye category. Why not Wild Turkey 101 Rye or Russell's Reserve Single Barrel Rye? Both are incredible representations of Wild Turkey's quality rye whiskey, but

Rare Breed Rye proved the most versatile of the bunch. One could argue each of the brand's rye expressions is perfect for cocktails, blending, or just plain neat sipping. Hell, I could argue that easily. But Rare Breed Rye . . . it just seems to work whenever and however I need it. It's also pretty damn bold any which way you sip it. If there's one Wild Turkey offering that never loses its edge, it's Rare Breed Rye.

Best Single Barrel (2021)
Single Cask Nation Wild Turkey
(Barrel #20-0202)

In a sea of single-barrel offerings, there's one label that immediately catches the eye, Single Cask Nation. I've been impressed with Joshua Hatton and Jason Johnstone-Yellin's "independent bottling company that could" since I first tasted their 2016 Whisky Jewbilee. J&J Spirits' Single Cask Nation is a brand loaded with unique, thought-provoking hits, and Wild Turkey barrel #20-0202 is surely one of them. Its distinctive fruity-herbal character is best summarized in the following excerpt from my July 2021 review:

> *If you've ever wondered what Fruity Pebbles might taste like as a whiskey, give this bourbon a try. The hard-to-place fruitiness is intense. It's not the everyday orange, cherry, or apple you find in Wild Turkey at this age. Instead, something funky, herbal, even tropical, is revealed. This is the type of barrel that stands out—one that's desired and remembered fondly when it's gone.*

Admittedly, I wasn't much of a rickhouse E bourbon fan when barrels first hit Wild Turkey's private selection program in 2020. But this Single

Cask Nation selection . . . This is something else. In fact, it's so atypical, fans of the familiar "core Turkey" profile might find themselves struggling for sure footing. Fortunately for me, I'm mesmerized by its syncopated intricacies and oddities. Single Cask Nation #20-0202 is a genuine stunner. It's not everyone's jam, but it's damn sure mine.

PATRON'S CHOICE (2021)
RUSSELL'S RESERVE SINGLE BARREL BOURBON

For the last two years I've asked my amazing Patreon supporters—my community of diehard Wild Turkey fanatics—which expression is their annual favorite. This year—well, let's just say there were no surprises. Russell's Reserve Single Barrel Bourbon holds tightly to its crown. In a crazy new world where Wild Turkey limited editions are nearly impossible to find, it's comforting to know that Russell's Reserve Single Barrel Bourbon is reasonably obtainable (fingers crossed). Be it the standard retail offering or single-barrel private selections, 110-proof, non-chill-filtered Wild Turkey for $65 is hard to pass up.

But if one were to focus solely on 2021 Russell's Reserve Single Barrel private selections, I'd have to say that McBrayer B selections were my overall favorite. There were winners from rickhouse K, F, and CNA (among various holdovers from 2019 and 2020), but McBrayer B offered something unexpected, a grape-like "crushable" profile uncommonly found in modern Wild Turkey. Whether or not my patrons agree with me, you'd have to ask them. But I'd wager most who have tasted the range of 2021 selections would.

BEST WHISKEY OVERALL (2021)
RUSSELL'S RESERVE
13 YEAR OLD BOURBON

There are three words that I can guarantee will either get you an emphatic "hell yes," or an exhaustive "sigh": Russell's Reserve Thirteen. We all knew it was coming, but what we didn't know is how insane the demand for Russell's Reserve 13-Year would be. That demand only drove an even more insane whiskey secondary market value, making the appropriately retail-priced expression ripe for profiteers and charlatans. Unsurprisingly, bad behavior continues to this day.

Shenanigans aside, Eddie Russell should be immensely proud of Russell's Reserve 13-Year. The artful combination of thirteen-year and nineteen-year bourbon—involving barrels from both the Camp Nelson and Tyrone campuses—is a whiskey tour de force. Credit should also be given to Wild Turkey's resident Food Scientist, Shaylyn Gammon, who assisted Eddie with dialing in the masterful batch using only her nose (Shaylyn was pregnant at the time). An undeniably impressive bourbon by an impressive team of talented individuals. Is it worth secondary valuations? Not to me. That said, Russell's Reserve 13-Year is better than a grand majority of whiskeys regularly flipped for significantly higher amounts. It's my whiskey of 2021, and it's likely many others' as well.

In a year of whiplash-inducing highs and lows, it's comforting to know that Wild Turkey (again) gave us quality whiskey to rely on. Some expressions were harder to find than others—one in particular that didn't make this list, Master's Keep One. I'll spare my defense of its exclusion but understand that it's okay for us to disagree on what's best. It's one of the things that makes whiskey enthusiasm a great hobby. If we all agreed on everything . . . *Where's the fun in that?*

With 2021 in the rearview mirror and 2022 on the horizon, I encourage everyone to look forward to brighter days. Will they arrive this coming year? It's hard to say; 2021 was arguably 2020 Part II. But it's always better to hope than despair.

As for Wild Turkey, I'm curious how its brands will evolve given the times. At present, Wild Turkey, Russell's Reserve, and Longbranch no longer share space on the same Wild Turkey website; each brand has its own. I believe it's safe to assume Wild Turkey will continue its present course. We'll see the same familiar bottles on shelves, so long as pandemic-related supply chain issues resolve. Russell's Reserve may release a second thirteen-year batch (please and thank you, Campari). And Longbranch . . . I believe McConaughey's baby is destined for expansion. It could be a rye whiskey; it could be a liqueur. Only time will tell. Regardless of what happens (or doesn't), I'll be eager to write about it. That, you can count on.

Cheers, and have a happy and safe 2022!

EPILOGUE

L ooking back on my first five years of writing about Wild Turkey, one thing strikes me more than any other: its uncanny revival in popularity. Reading through my early posts, it's as if I'm struggling to convince readers to give Wild Turkey a fair shake. By the time you reach 2020, the tone has shifted, and even more so by 2021, when the topics turn to addressing FOMO and avoiding the many pitfalls of the whiskey secondary markets. It appears that good behavior surrounding the legendary brand's expressions is encouraged almost as much as trying the expressions themselves.

One could argue this is a positive thing for American whiskey, particularly bourbon; moreover, one could argue it's a positive thing for Wild Turkey. Hopefully, it is, though I have my periodic doubts. What's most important is that we, as consumers, recognize the intrinsic value of whiskey: a spirit crafted to be enjoyed, savored, and shared. Bottle sales fueled by hype and scarcity seldom justify monetary outlay after the cork is popped and the contents emptied. What's left are priceless memories, experience, and recognition of the moment.

Thankfully, it doesn't take a thousand-dollar bottle to leave a lasting impression. I've been fortunate enough to taste Wild Turkey spanning the 1950s to today, and I've had equally rewarding experiences rooted in each decade.

As this retrospective comes to an end, I ask one thing of you: reflect on what truly makes you happy in regard to whiskey appreciation. Is it the acquisition of rare, sought-after bottles? If you're solely a collector, maybe that's an appropriate answer. That being said, I'd wager most of you reading cherish the liquid over the glass. And if that's the case, know that there should always be an affordable, quality bottle of Wild Turkey within your reach.

Cheers and all the best!

WILD TURKEY TIMELINE
(* = APPROXIMATE TIME)

1830*: Brothers James and John Ripy (French Huguenot descendants) arrive in America from Ireland.

1840-1850*: The Ripy family opens a general store in Tyrone, KY (named in honor of Tyrone, Ireland).

1850: Fitts, Martin & Clough is established as a wholesale grocer in New York, NY.

1850–1859*: A distillery operating as Old Moore is built in Tyrone, KY, in the general area that would eventually become Wild Turkey Distillery.

1855: Fitts, Martin & Clough is reorganized as Fitts & Turner.

1861: Robert F. Austin joins the firm of Fitts & Turner resulting in Fitts, Austin & Turner.

1862–1864: Fitts, Austin & Turner is reorganized as Fitts & Austin.

1869: Thomas Beebe "T.B." Ripy (youngest son of James Ripy) begins distilling whiskey at Cliff Springs Distillery in Tyrone, KY.

1872: James Ripy dies.

1873: T.B. Ripy builds a new distillery, increasing capacity from 600 bushels to over 1,200 bushels per day.

1878–1879: James E. Nichols purchases an interest in Fitts & Austin (formerly Fitts, Austin & Turner) resulting in the creation of Austin, Nichols & Co.

1881: T.B. Ripy partners with J.M. Waterfill and John Dowling to build the Clover Bottom Distillery in Tyrone, KY.

1883–1885: T.B. Ripy acquires ownership of additional Kentucky distilleries, including Belle of Anderson Distillery and Old Joe Distillery.

1885: T.B. Ripy buys out his partners and becomes the sole owner of Clover Bottom Distillery; production increases to 1,500 bushels per day.

1888: James P. Ripy (brother of T.B. Ripy) purchases the Old Moore Distillery in Tyrone, KY from J.W. Stephens; the construction of T.B. Ripy's Queen Anne style mansion is completed.

1891: Old Moore Distillery is demolished and replaced by a new distillery, Old Hickory Springs; James P. Ripy partners with Ike Bernheim and production of J.P. Ripy whiskey begins.

1893: T.B. Ripy's whiskey is selected from over 400 whiskeys to represent the state of Kentucky at the World's Fair Exposition in Chicago, IL.

1902: T.B. Ripy dies; his distilleries are assimilated into the Kentucky Distilleries and Warehouse Co. (AKA the Whiskey Trust).

1905: T.B. Ripy's sons purchase the Old Hickory Springs Distillery site from their uncle, James P. Ripy, and establish Ripy Brothers Distillery.

1919: The 18th Amendment (Prohibition) puts an end to many distilleries, including the Kentucky Distilleries and Warehouse Co. and Ripy Brothers Distillery.

1933: The 21st Amendment (Repeal of Prohibition) enables the Ripy family to restore and rebuild the distillery located on their property.

1934: Austin, Nichols & Co. enters the wine and spirits industry.

1935*: Construction of the new Ripy Brothers Distillery is completed in Lawrenceburg, KY; the Ripys begin to produce whiskey under contract; the Old Ripy whiskey brand (now a property of Schenley Distillers) is introduced.

1939: Austin, Nichols & Co. ceases grocery distribution and shifts all resources to wine and spirits sales.

1940: Austin, Nichols executive Thomas McCarthy envisions the Wild Turkey brand and its signature 101 proof; Ripy Brothers Distillery enters into a production agreement with Schenley Distillers.

1942: Austin, Nichols & Co. markets Wild Turkey 101 Bourbon sourced from Ripy Bros. and several other Kentucky distilleries (likely Old Boone, Old Joe, Barton, Beam, Bernheim, and/or Schenley).

1949: Alvin and Robert Gould purchase the Ripy Brothers Distillery.

1950: Ripy Brothers Distillery is renamed Anderson County Distilling Co.

1950*: Wild Turkey 101 Rye sourced from Baltimore Pure Rye in Maryland (mash bill is reportedly 65% rye, 23% corn, 12% barley, or possibly 98% rye, 2% barley).

1954: Jimmy Russell begins employment at Anderson County Distilling Co.

1955: Anderson County Distilling Co. is renamed J.T.S. Brown & Sons.

1958–1959: Wild Turkey labels are changed from Brooklyn, NY to New York, NY.

1960*: Wild Turkey 101 Rye sourced from Michter's/Pennco in Pennsylvania (confirmed mash bill is 65% rye, 23% corn, 12% barley); Supplementary rye sourced from Maryland and Illinois through at least 1979.

1967: Jimmy Russell is promoted to Master Distiller at J.T.S. Brown & Sons.

1969: Liggett Myers Tobacco Co. acquires Austin, Nichols & Co.

1971: Austin, Nichols & Co. purchases the J.T.S. Brown & Sons Distillery (now Wild Turkey Distillery) in Lawrenceburg, KY; the first series of Wild Turkey decanters are produced.

1972: Wild Turkey labels are changed from New York, NY to Lawrenceburg, KY.

PRIOR TO 1973: Wild Turkey bourbon at 86.8 proof is introduced.

1974: Wild Turkey bourbon at 80 proof is introduced.

1974*: Wild Turkey 101 rye distillation is moved to Lawrenceburg, KY (the mash bill is changed to a reported 52% rye, 36% corn, 12% barley).

1976: Wild Turkey Liqueur (presently known as Wild Turkey American Honey) is introduced; Wild Turkey acquires five rickhouses in McBrayer from Four Roses Distillery.

1980: Austin, Nichols & Co. is purchased by Pernod Ricard from Liggett Myers Tobacco Co.

1980*: Wild Turkey "Beyond Duplication" 101 12-year bourbon is released.

1981: Eddie Russell begins work at Wild Turkey as a relief operator (Eddie states his actual title as "General Helper").

1984: The first steel fermentation tank is installed at Austin, Nichols Distilling Co., thus beginning the phaseout of cypress tanks (by the mid-1990s, only steel fermentation tanks would be used by Wild Turkey).

1985*: Wild Turkey 101 12-Year bourbon changes to the "Cheesy Gold Foil" label for the domestic market.

1985: Boulevard Distillers & Importers, Inc. files with the Kentucky Secretary of State as an FCO (foreign corporation); Austin, Nichols' parent company, Pernod Ricard, begins using "Boulevard Distillers" as a trade name for Wild Turkey.

1988*: Wild Turkey 101 12-Year Cuvee Lafayette is released exclusively in France.

1989: The last series of Wild Turkey decanters are produced.

1991: Wild Turkey Rare Breed is introduced, the first batch being "W-T-01-91."

1991*: Wild Turkey Kentucky Legend (non-age-stated, 101-proof bourbon) is released as a duty-free exclusive.

1992: Wild Turkey 101 8-Year bourbon loses its age statement domestically and is reintroduced as Wild Turkey "Old No.8 Brand" (Wild Turkey 101/8 continues to be released outside the U.S., its glass is embossed with an "8 Years Old"); 1855 Reserve ("From the Makers of Wild Turkey") is released to foreign markets, the first batch being "W-T-01-92."

1992*: Wild Turkey 101 12-Year bourbon changes to a "Split Label" design for the domestic market.

1994: Wild Turkey Kentucky Spirit is released with its signature pewter top; Wild Turkey Tradition (non-age-stated, 101 proof) replaces the duty-free Wild Turkey Kentucky Legend (see 1991).

1996: 1855 Reserve discontinued, the last batch being W-T-01-96; Wild Turkey runs low on warehouse space and begins storing barrels in the brick rickhouses of the former Old Taylor Distillery (Stone Castle).

1998*: Wild Turkey Kentucky Legend (single barrel at barrel proof, AKA "Donut") is released as a duty-free expression.

1999: Wild Turkey labels are changed from a forward-facing turkey to a turkey in profile; the use of "Old No.8 Brand" on Wild Turkey 101 labels ends; Wild Turkey Rare Breed labels are redesigned to include a turkey.

1999*: Wild Turkey 101 12-Year bourbon is discontinued domestically; Wild Turkey 101/12 continues as an export with a "Pseudo-Split" label (Turkey "in profile").

2000: A fire destroys Warehouse J at Wild Turkey in Lawrenceburg, Kentucky; bottling moves to Lawrenceburg, Indiana (a Pernod Ricard facility).

2001: Wild Turkey Russell's Reserve (ten-year bourbon at 101 proof) is introduced; Wild Turkey 101 17-Year bourbon is released in Japan.

2002: Wild Turkey Freedom (non-age-stated, 106-proof bourbon) is released as a duty-free exclusive; Wild Turkey Kentucky Spirit stoppers are changed from pewter to dark wood.

2003*: The official Wild Turkey web URL is added to bottle labels.

2004: Barrel-entry proof changes from 107 to 110 for both mash bills (bourbon and rye); Wild Turkey Tribute fifteen-year bourbon released (101 proof in the U.S.; 110 proof in Japan).

2005: Russell's Reserve 10-Year bourbon (90 proof) is introduced; Wild Turkey Heritage (a single-barrel bourbon at 101 proof) is released as a duty-free exclusive; Wild Turkey Kentucky Spirit cork caps are engraved with the Wild Turkey logo.

2006: Barrel-entry proof changes from 110 to 115 for both mash bills (bourbon and rye); bottling moves to Fort Smith, Arkansas; Wild Turkey Master Distiller's Selection fourteen-year bourbon released in Japan; Wild Turkey Liqueur is reintroduced as Wild Turkey American Honey; Russell's Reserve bottles filled at Fort Smith, AR are embossed with "Jimmy Russell."

PRIOR TO 2006: Wild Turkey 101 12-Year bourbon export label changes from "Pseudo-Split" to a "Uni-label."

2007: Russell's Reserve 6-Year rye is introduced; Wild Turkey American Spirit, a fifteen-year bottled-in-bond bourbon, is released.

2008: Eddie Russell named Associate Master Distiller.

2008*: Wild Turkey Kentucky Spirit cork caps changed from dark engraved wood to light engraved wood.

2009: Gruppo Campari purchases the Wild Turkey brand; Austin, Nichols & Co. is retained by Pernod Ricard; Austin, Nichols Distilling Co. continues as an assumed name of Campari; Russell's Reserve labels are changed to a paper strip design; Wild Turkey Tradition fourteen-year bourbon is released.

2010: The remaining barrels stored at the former Old Taylor Distillery (Stone Castle) are moved back to Wild Turkey (about 80,000 barrels of different ages had been matured at Old Taylor from 1996 to 2010).

2011: The new Wild Turkey Distillery begins operations in Lawrenceburg, KY, and replaces the old Austin, Nichols/ Boulevard/Anderson County/Ripy Bros. Distillery; Wild Turkey labels change from a full-color turkey "in profile" to a monochrome (sepia toned) turkey "in profile;" the name "Austin, Nichols" becomes less prominent on Wild Turkey labels; Wild Turkey 81 replaces Wild Turkey 80-proof bourbon.

2012: Wild Turkey Rye (81 proof) is introduced; Wild Turkey 101 Rye is allocated to limited distribution.

2013: Russell's Reserve Single Barrel Bourbon (non-age-stated at 110 proof) is introduced; bottling returns to Lawrenceburg, KY; Wild Turkey 101 12-Year bourbon (export) is discontinued; Wild Turkey 13-Year Distiller's Reserve is released as an export-only expression; Wild Turkey Forgiven (batch #302) is released.

2014: Wild Turkey Diamond Anniversary, American Honey Sting, and Wild Turkey Forgiven (batch #303) are released; Wild Turkey 101 Rye distribution is increased (primarily as liter bottles); the Wild Turkey Visitor Center (informally dubbed "Cathedral to Bourbon") opens to the public.

2015: Eddie Russell named Master Distiller; Bruce Russell begins as Brand Ambassador; Wild Turkey labels are changed from a monochrome turkey "in profile" to a redesigned larger black and white sketched turkey; Russell's Reserve labels are changed to a larger "rustic" design; Russell's Reserve Single Barrel Rye introduced; Wild Turkey Master's Keep 17-Year and Russell's Reserve 1998 are released as limited editions.

2016: Matthew McConaughey hired as Creative Director for Wild Turkey.

2017: Wild Turkey Master's Keep Decades is released; Campari Whiskey Barons Old Ripy and Bond & Lillard (produced by Wild Turkey) are released in limited distribution; Wild Turkey Master's Keep 1894 is released as an Australian exclusive; Rare Breed's bottle shape is redesigned with its label displaying the new black and white sketched turkey (see 2015); Jimmy Russell's granddaughter, JoAnn Street, joins the Wild Turkey team as a distillery tour guide and brand ambassador.

2018: Wild Turkey Longbranch, a bourbon collaboration between Creative Director Matthew McConaughey and Master Distiller Eddie Russell is introduced; Wild Turkey Master's Keep Revival, a twelve- to fifteen-year bourbon finished in Spanish ex-Oloroso-Sherry casks, is released; Russell's Reserve 2002 is released as an allocated limited edition.

2019: Bruce Russell named Global Brand Ambassador for Wild Turkey; Campari Whiskey Barons W.B. Saffell and Bond & Lillard batch #2 (reportedly distilled by Wild Turkey under Eddie Russell's supervision) are released nationwide; Wild Turkey Kentucky Spirit's iconic "turkey tail feather" bottle is discontinued and replaced with a design similar to Rare Breed; Wild Turkey Master's Keep Cornerstone, the distillery's first limited-edition rye whiskey, is released; Russell's Reserve Single Barrel Bourbon private selection bottles receive a new set of labels (back/front) stating barrel maturation location, dates of distillation and bottling.

2020: Wild Turkey Master's Keep Bottled in Bond, a seventeen-year straight bourbon aged in Camp Nelson's rickhouses, is released; Wild Turkey Rare Breed Rye makes its debut at 112.2 proof (NCF); Longbranch becomes a unique brand of Wild Turkey; Russell's Reserve 2003 is released as an allocated limited edition; a new "embossed Turkey" bottle design for Wild Turkey 101 makes its debut in 1.75l bottles.

2021: Wild Turkey 101 Rye available in 750ml bottles for the first time since 2011; Russell's Reserve 13-Year bourbon makes its debut at 114.8 proof (NCF); Master's Keep One, the brand's first whiskey to feature a toasted oak secondary maturation, is released.

BIBLIOGRAPHY

Bourbon Pursuit. (Various interviews with the Russells). http://bourbonpursuit.com.

Campari America (official website). http://camparigroup.com.

Cowdery, Charles K. *Bourbon, Straight—The Uncut and Unfiltered Story of American Whiskey*. Made and Bottled in Kentucky, Chicago, IL: 2004.

Cowdery, Charles K. *Bourbon, Strange—Surprising Stories of American Whiskey*. Made and Bottled in Kentucky, Chicago, IL: 2014.

Cowdery, Charles K. "Wild Turkey Unveils New Distillery." The Chuck Cowdery Blog. http://chuckcowdery.blogspot.com: June 21, 2011

Goldfarb, Aaron. *Hacking Whiskey: Smoking, Blending, Fat Washing, and Other Whiskey Experiments*. Dovetail Press, Brooklyn, NY: 2018.

Historical Research Associates, Inc. *Wild Turkey Visitor Center: Historical Materials*. March 15, 2013.

Lexico.com. https://www.lexico.com/en/definition/cornerstone. Retrieved: April 13, 2019

Lexico.com. https://www.lexico.com/en/definition/golden_age. Retrieved: April 17, 2018

Lipman, John F. "The Boulevard Distilling Company." American Whiskey. http://ellenjaye.com: March 30, 2011.

Merriam-Webster.com. https://www.merriam-webster.com/dictionary/golden%20age. Retrieved: April 17, 2018.

Minnick, Fred. *Bourbon Curious—A Simple Tasting Guide for the Savvy Drinker*. Zenith Press, Minneapolis, MN: 2015.

Minnick, Fred. *Bourbon—The Rise, Fall, and Rebirth of an American Whiskey*. Voyageur Publishing, Minneapolis, MN: 2016.

One Nation Under Whisky. (Various interviews with the Russells). http://onenationunderwhisky.com

Pre-Pro.com. http://pre-pro.com.

Risen, Clay. *American Whiskey, Bourbon & Rye*. Sterling Epicure, New York, NY: 2013.

University of Kentucky—Nunn Center. (Various interviews with the Ripy and Russell families). https://www.youtube.com/user/nunncenter: 2014.

Veach, Michael R. "Old Bottle Bourbon Flavor." BourbonVeach.com: Bourbon History. https://bourbonveach.com/2016/10/03/old-bottle-bourbon-flavor: October 3, 2016

Whiskey ID. http://whiskeyid.com.

Wild Turkey Bourbon (official website). http://wildturkeybourbon.com.

"Wild Turkey Master's Keep 1894." The Whisky Ledger. http://whisky-ledger.com: August 3, 2017.

Young, Al. *Four Roses: The Return of a Whiskey Legend*. Butler Books, Louisville, KY: 2013.

Acknowledgments

Were it not for the support of my readers, *Wild Turkey Musings* wouldn't exist. The pages ahead bear the names of many generous individuals who have contributed to the *Rare Bird 101* blog via Patreon, as well as this book's Kickstarter campaign. I have other individuals and entities to thank and will endeavor to do so without leaving anyone out.

Thanks to Wild Turkey and Campari, especially Sean Hudgins, Duffey Sida, Frank Dudley, Amy McClam, and Bo Garrett, for seeing value in my work and for understanding my passion and motivation. Watching the brand grow over the years has been a marvelous adventure. I have confidence things can only get better.

To the Russell family—Jimmy, Eddie, Bruce, and JoAnn—words cannot express the level of admiration and respect I have for your humility and professionalism. Three generations of uncompromising dedication . . . here's to many more!

Special thanks to Fred Minnick, who's never failed to lend a hand throughout my whiskey writing journey. You're a busy man, Fred, and I truly appreciate you taking the time to entertain my inquiries. (You also wrote a kick-ass foreword.)

To Dom Alcocer, Stacey Beerman, Sarah Bessette, Dave Ensler, Dave Karraker, and Allison Pinkston, all of you fine professionals have assisted me in invaluable ways. And though you've all moved on from Wild Turkey, we still cross paths from time to time. It's always a pleasure. Thank you.

I'd like to dedicate a few sentences to Chuck Cowdery. Chuck, were it not for your blog, I probably would've never started one myself. You have a way with words. Your points, your pace, and your seemingly effortless transitions to drill into the heart of the matter always grant me a smile and a chuckle. Even at your most terse, you're profound. It's the damnedest thing. Not to mention, your body of work is a resource unrivaled. I sincerely hope your articles are archived for future generations.

To Chris Toner and Aaron Goldfarb, each of you played a unique and equally important part in making my blog, and eventually this book, a reality. I can't thank y'all enough.

Who's the greatest Wild Turkey fan in the world? Don't look at me. That honor belongs to David James. David, your knowledge and generosity is unmatched. I'm grateful for your friendship, wisdom, and honest perspective in today's "world gone mad" whiskey times. You don't just talk about what makes this hobby great, you live it. I'm not sure I'll ever be able to repay your kindness, but I'll make it a goal to see it's never lost or forgotten.

To Ricky Frame, Victor Sizemore, Connor Query, Taylor Cope, Julia Steffy, Brandon Coward, and the entire team at Mascot Books—I appreciate your skill and attention to detail. Just look at this book! I couldn't be more proud. Incredible.

Special thanks to Ryan Alves and Justins' House of Bourbon for providing some of the rarer bottles photographed for *Wild Turkey Musings*. Thanks as well to John Henderson for keeping my websites running smoothly and to Jay West for being an excellent springboard (or occasional brick wall) for my crazy ideas.

To all of my family and friends who encourage me daily, my sincerest gratitude. And to my best friend and devoted wife, Kim, and my amazing children, Roan and Finley: know that I cherish your help and support. You inspire me daily and give me confidence when it's hard to find. You're the best part of my life, and I'm forever grateful.

DAVID JENNINGS

Special thanks to the following:

BENEFACTORS ELITE

Ryan Alves

Roger A. Conant

Taylor Cope

Mike Cunningham

Jon Gunderson

Carl Pogoncheff

James Richards

BENEFACTORS

Andrew Brewer

Argesarge

Braxton Underwood

Brett K. Anderson

Brian Johnson

Carroll Stang

Clark Kebodeaux

Corey Margason

David James

David Stanley

Dennis Weedman

Donnie Webb

Dylan Buras

Edward Bell

Elliott Patrick

Ernest Jack Johnson

Evan Young

Goshenman

James Fletcher

Joe Lara

John Zilg

Jonathan Cane

Joseph Alan Doll

Josh Lozner

Kerry Bossak

Kevin Palczynski

Kevin Williams

Lance Robinson

Lee Barkalow

Mark Saylor

Matt Kusek

Michael Comerford

Michael Williams

Nick Granado

Nick Thompson

Nullius

Paul Bell

Paul Davis

Paul Marko

Peter Braddock

Phil Kollin

Ralph Mittl

Robert Warren

Scott Forosisky

Stephen Mansfield

Sterling DeMasters

Steve Dickson

Steve Porter

Steve Swain

Steven Ury

Terry Gilman

T.J. Thompson

Travis Allen-Jacob Spees

Wes Milligan

BACKERS I

Aaron Konen
Allan Channell
Brad Vermeersch
Brandon
Christine Deems
Cody Burk
David C. Williard
David R. Proffitt
David Scarlett
Dunnnaway
Eduardo Aguirre
Eric Fabian
Erin Russell
Jeffrey Ball
Jessica
John Hughes
Jonathan Wilson
Joshua Case
Justin Massman
Masaki Sugimoto
Michael Langston
Patrick Nall
Schocking
Scott Pigsley
Shane Lott
Shem Coward
Tanya Thompson
Topher Kohan
Wade Bemis
William McMahon

BACKERS II

Aaron Marchut Lavallee
A.J. Zelenak
Andrew Chun
Andrew Dodd
Christopher Stormer
Don Hamilton
Eddie
Eduardo Medina
Frank Dobbins
James W. DeClue
Jeff Andersen
Jeff Pontius
John Robertson
Jon Ashbaugh
Jonathan Maisano
Josh Rice
Justin Jenkins
Kenny Coleman
Mathew Sims
Nate Russell
Nicholas
Ray Chappel
Richard Cannon
Ryan Adams
Tyler Thompson
Zachary Wisniewski

PATRONS

Aaron Artino
Aaron Blizzard
Aaron Goldfarb
Aaron Johnson
Aaron Konen
Aaron Lalonde
Aaron Marchant
Aaron Melamed
Adam Glover
Adam Husted
Adam Jay
Adam Runyan
Adam Shelton
Adam Terry
Adam Wakeland
Adam Winter
Adilio Samuels
Alan Corey
Alan Guseilo
Alec Johnston
Alex Kitchens
Alex Klapp
Alex Piehl
Alexander McCabe
Ali Mashhoon
Alpay Temiz
Amenawon Ogiefo
Anders Larson
Andrew Brewer
Andrew Chun

Andrew Derousseau
Andrew Dinger
Andrew Dodd
Andrew Galvin
Andrew Jerdonek
Andrew Maroney
Andrew Mattson
Andrew Pawlowski
Andy Southworth
Anthony Girardi
Anthony Holstein
Aras Naujokas
Ashton Walters
Austin
Austin Dodson
Austin Felts
Austin Joiner
Austin Sims
Avi Wells
Azi Katz
Beau Beatty
Ben Adams
Ben Hankins
Ben Pickett
Benjamin Kneeland
Benny Hurwitz
Billy Atwood
Billy Belsom
Blake Barbaresi
Blake Park

Blake Potter
Blake Ross
Brad Fields
Braden Johnson
Bradley Adams
Bradley Westendorf
Brandon Duckworth
Brandon Griffiths
Brandon Lima
Braxton Underwood
Brent Michener
Brent Ray
Bret Ginter
Brett Mitsch
Brian Allen
Brian Beyke
Brian Franklin
Brian Girard
Brian Henning
Brian Johnson
Brian Lauer
Brian Lowe
Brian Sand
Brian Schild
Brian Vitale
Brint Roden
Britton Smith
Bryan Brantley
Bryan Jordan
Bryan Sacadat

Bryant Roberts
Burt Tsuchiya
Cameron Pate
Cameron Sattenfield
Carps
Carroll Lee Stang
Carson Marino
Cary Mauk
Chad Holley
Chad Johnson
Chad Lewis
Chad McKibben
Charles Fox
Charles Gaddy
Chris Banham
Chris Blue
Chris Cameron
Chris Cheng
Chris Decker
Chris Ford
Chris Harris
Chris Lynn
Chris Rickey
Chris Sebastian
Chris Shock
Chris W.
Chris Woods
Christian Badali
Christian Winters
Christine Glasheen
Christopher Barcinas
Christopher Clepp
Christopher Collazo
Christopher Donelson
Christopher Nelson
Christopher Stormer
Chuck Cole

Chuck Crotts
Clark Kebodeaux
Clay Grier
Clay Kesterson
Clay Miller
Clay Monroe
Clayton Vermeire
Cody Burkholder
Cody Deskins
Cody Wierck
Colby Binford
Colin Larsgaard
Colin McDonough
Connor Slein
Curt Kolcun
Curtis Ritchie
Dale Console
Dan Gryson
Dan Hendricks
Dan Smith
Dane Lickteig
Daniel
Daniel Blair
Daniel Chong
Daniel Glover
Daniel Heun
Daniel L Fleck
Daniel Lavender
Daniel Viaches
Danny Carter
Darin Mast
Darren Wright
Darryl Jessup
Dave Friedman
David A. James
David Barnes
David C. Williard

David Cahoe
David Hofmann
David Killion
David Marra
David Qin
David Sadler
David Schimizzi
David Schweibold
David Stanley
David Sugg
David Sullivan
David Terebessy
Dennis Drinkwater
Dennis Weedman
Derek Laverriere
Dillon McKenzie-Veal
Donnie Webb
Donny Engell
Douglas Carlson
Dustin Finner
Dustin Stone
Dylan Buras
E. D. Jack Johnson
Eduardo Medina
Edward Andrew
Lawrence
Edward Bell
Elijah James Poferl
Elliott Patrick
Eric Elmer
Eric Fabian
Eric Fela
Eric Janssen
Eric larson
Eric Olson
Eric Simpson
Eric Spielman

Eric Stumbo
Eric Thomas
Erik Rothschild
Erik Sponholz
Erik Wehling
Erin Walsh
Erjon Dega
Ernie Escontrias
Ethan Turk
Evan Belt
Evan Branscum
Evan Favocci
Evan Nordgren
Evan Young
Fletcher Gonzalez
Forrest McMillan
Fred Gilbert
Freda Kohler
Fritz Gutwein
Gabe Zuccarelli
Garn Miller
George Ryan Connor
George W. A. Duncan
Gerald Jennings
Grant Ahten
Greg West
Gregory Lopez
H. Lee Delaney
Harold Broughton
Hayne Begley
Heather Keller
Himrajh Ali, Jr.
Ian Andrews
Ian Pointer
Ian Steidel
Ignacio Solares
J.D. Ley

Jack Parker
Jackson Eldridge
Jacob Armbrecht
Jacob Kiper
Jacob Knight
Jacob M. Runge
Jacob Springman
Jacob Wheeler
Jake Wessel
James Ashcraft
James Brian
James Brian Anderson
James Dellinger
James Dicks
James Richards
James Sanderson
James Skidmore
James Smythe
Jamie Baalmann
Jamy Deutch
Jared Compton
Jared Noffsinger
Jared Reeves
Jason Bible
Jason Blanchard
Jason Braswell
Jason Burnett
Jason Callori
Jason Flegm
Jason Goldberger
Jason Kinzey
Jason Martini
Jason Price
Jason Snodgress
Jason Wayne
Jay Alvarez
Jay West

Jeff Berner
Jeff Boren
Jeff Pontius
Jeffrey Jankovich
Jeffrey Ventimiglia
Jeremy Jackson
Jeremy Kustoff
Jerry Castleberry
Jim B.
Jim Fraser
Jim Shannon
Joe Abello
Joel Francis
Joel Price Jr
John Bailey
John Belmont
John Haley
John Henderson
John Pedlow
John Prieto
John Rachuy, II
John Reintjes
John Robertson
John Shelton
John Sobotowski
John Street
John T. Cabrera
John Wadsworth
Jon
Jon Kines
Jon Raney
Jon Warner
Jonas Chaudhary
Jonathan Ashbaugh
Jonathan Mason
Jonathan Smith
Jonathan Watson

Jonathon Davis	Justin McGill	Lincoln Hammons
Jonathon Mahle	Justin Paquette	Liz Mutschler
Jordan C. Fay	Justin Whitfield	Logan Ballew
Jordan Delmundo	Keith Gray	Logan Hayden
Jordan Ideker	Keith Little	Logan Kaptis
Jordan Reaves	Keith Schmidt	Lonnie Ennis
Jordan VandeBogart	Ken Barth	Lukas Baner
Jordan Welker	Ken Bodek	Luke Nortz
Jose Cruz Bueno, Jr.	Ken Carlsen	Luke Van Nek
Jose Saint Esteben	Kenneth Hamlet	Luke W. Cuculis
Jose Santiago	Kenny Coleman	Malt Review
Joseph G. Dunn	Kevin Anthony Lenau	Marcelo Kurtz
Joseph Hunter Zeppa	Kevin Berkowitz	Marcus Metzger
Joseph Nantz	Kevin Dawson	Marcus Sepanski
Joseph Schad	Kevin Eaton	Mark A. Smith
Joseph Van Nausdle	Kevin O'Connor	Mark Bologna
Josh Clark	Kevin Ogan	Mark Bylok
Josh Enneking	Kevin Palczynski	Mark Dickinson
Josh Kelley	Kevin Williams	Mark Guagenti
Josh LaRoque	Kiefer Johnson	Mark Linder
Josh londergan	Kim Michael	Mark McNul
Josh Lozner	Kirby Novacek	Mark Tompkins
Josh Peters	Kolte Bowers	Mark Tribendis
Josh Randall	Kyle Anderson	Marsha Hanners
Josh Rosenholtz	Kyle Denny	Marvin Coleman, Jr.
Josh Salyer	Kyle P. Cull	Mathew Houchens
Joshua D. Smith	Kyle Ragsdale	Matt Cline
Joshua Hatton	Kyle Shiparski	Matt Ewens
Joshua Hauger	Lance Lyell	Matt Greene
Joshua Shupp	Larry Hart	Matt Holbrook
Joshua Smith	Lee Barkalow	Matt Luccarelli
Joshua Walker	Lee Provoost	Matt Mace
Justin Alford	Leio Heyenrath	Matt Michael
Justin Brad Wilson	Leo Titus	Matt Simmons
Justin Brokaw	Levi Stamer	Matthew Hoffman
Justin D. Jenkins	Levi Van Dyke	Matthew Koeth
Justin Jacobson	Lewis Joline	Matthew Layton

Matthew OBrien

Matthew Peters

Matthew Piccorelli

Matthew Purnell

Matthew Tischler

Matthew Weaver

Matthew Webb

Max Schockett

Meilech Prero

Micah Wong

Michael Alex Stroud

Michael Andrew Clark

Michael Copeland

Michael Cornet

Michael Harrison

Michael J. Thompson

Michael K. Porter

Michael Lambright

Michael Marino

Michael Mertens

Michael Mongelluzzo

Michael Smith

Michael Smolanoff

Michael Woodruff

Miguel Aleman

Miguel Perez

Mike

Mike Comerford

Mike Czyzewski

Mike Laumb

Mike Merritt

Mike Turdo

Mikey Conrad

Mikey Mudd

Miklos Gyorgy

Mitchell Bowman

Mitchell Burney

Molly Smith

Nate Gordon

Nathan Heskew

Nathan Lowe

Neal Stringer

Nellie Kuh

Nicholas Folmer

Nicholas Gilpin

Nicholas Mace

Nicholas Villaggio

Nick Baker

Nick Castiglione

Nick Combs

Nick Granado

Nick Hill

Nick Thompson

Nickoles Clason

Noah Wong

Patrick Earls

Patrick Garrett

Patrick Hermiller

Patrick Malchow

Paul Bell

Paul Davis

Paul Lafontaine

Paul Reeves

Pedro Zamora

Perry Ritter

Pete Schmidt

Peter Clausen

Phil Kollin

Philip Hand

Phillip Ray Mathis

Quenton

Ralph Mittl

Ramon Ontiveroz

Ray Cox

Raymond Shepard

Reid Bechtle

Rey E. Guerra

Rhett Morgan

Ric Peden

Richard Cannon

Richard Zicchino

Rick Chlopan

Ritesh Tripathi

RJ Otsuji

Rob Clark

Rob McCarthy

Rob Militzer

Robert S. Bigger

Robert Travis Haney

Robert Warren

Roger A. Conant

Ron Summers

Ross Retzler

Rudy Munoz

Russell Beck

Russell Hubbard

Ryan Alves

Ryan Buse

Ryan C. Adams

Ryan Cooley

Ryan Goethe

Ryan Herubin

Ryan Nelson

Ryan Pointer

Ryan Russell

Ryan Wester

Sam Ferruolo

Sam Kleinman

Samantha Stitt

Samer Musallam

Samuel Cason

Scott Bailey
Scott Early
Scott Forosisky
Scott Hill
Scott Marsden
Scott Peth
Scott Smart
Scott Tilton
Scott Tyson
Sean Crain
Sean Huebotter
Shane Hinkle
Shaowei Toh
Shaun Blake
Shawn Mcclung
Shem Coward
Stephen Benson
Stephen Carter
Stephen Mallory
Stephen Zimmer
Stephen Zittrouer
Sterling DeMasters
Steve Dickson
Steve Friedmann
Steve Swain
Steven A. Spear
Steven Dorman
Steven Porter
Stuart Katz
Stuart Schwab
Sungjin Park
T. A. Johns
Tanner Brown
Taylor Cope
The Bourbon
Boulevardier
Thomas Bianco

Thomas Gore
Thomas White
Tim Miller
Tim Sweeney
Timothy Ton-Estelle
T.J. Thompson
Todd Harrell
Tom Spear
Tony Freund
Tony Watson
Toyi Beguedou
Travis Allison
Travis Gault
Travis Widick
Trenton Morris
Tresmon Smith
Trevor A. Jarrait
Trevor Boyd
Troy Aydell
Tyler Ackerman
Tyler McKay Barnett
Tyler Sims
Tyler Trew
Tyler Wells
Voltz
W. K. Bleibel
Walker T. Candler, Jr.
Warren Hood
Wes Milligan
Wes Morris
Wesley Berger
Whiskey Knows
Will Henderson
William Burkhardt
William Edwards
William J. Wiley
William Mancia

William McMahon
William Price
William W. Hines
William West
Yan Shen
Zachary C. Hobbs
Zachary VanFleteren
Zaiyan Wei

ABOUT THE AUTHOR

David Jennings is a devout whiskey enthusiast and Wild Turkey superfan. In 2020, he authored *American Spirit: Wild Turkey Bourbon from Ripy to Russell* (Mascot Books), the definitive guide to Wild Turkey, its history, brands, and expressions. David lives in South Carolina with his wife and two children and writes about Wild Turkey bourbon and rye whiskey on his blog, *Rare Bird 101*.

Give David a follow at:

RareBird101.com | Instagram: @RBird101 | Twitter: @RBird101 | Patreon.com/RareBird101

About the Photographer

Victor Sizemore is a dedicated artist—traveling the globe in pursuit of the finest imagery. Over the last seventeen years, Victor has worked with the most recognized names in the spirits industry. His photography has been featured in *Bourbon Plus Magazine*, *The Bourbon Review*, and *Whisky Advocate*, as well as countless advertisements and social media campaigns.

Give Victor a follow at:

VictorSizemore.com | Instagram: @victorsizemore

MASCOT
BOOKS
an imprint of Amplify Publishing Group

www.amplifypublishinggroup.com

Wild Turkey Musings: A Whiskey Writer's Retrospective
©2023 David Jennings. All Rights Reserved. No part of this publication may be reproduced, stored in a retrieval system or transmitted in any form by any means electronic, mechanical, or photocopying, recording or otherwise without the permission of the author.

WILD TURKEY is a registered trademark of Campari America. This book is not authorized or produced by Wild Turkey Distillery or Campari America.

All photography by Victor Sizemore unless otherwise stated.
Book design and additional graphics by Ricky Frame.
Map paintings by Connor Query.

For more information, please contact:
Mascot Books, an imprint of Amplify Publishing Group
620 Herndon Parkway #320
Herndon, VA 20170
info@amplifypublishing.com

Library of Congress Control Number: 2022901987
CPSIA Code: PRV0922A
ISBN-13: 978-1-63755-491-3
Printed in the United States